Rubik's®

PUZZLES

101 PUZZLES TO TEST
YOUR BRAIN POWER

First edition for the United States, its territories and dependencies, and Canada published in 2018 by Barron's Educational Series, Inc.

Puzzles copyright © 2017 Carlton Books Limited

All inquiries should be addressed to:
Barron's Educational Series, Inc.
250 Wireless Boulevard
Hauppauge, NY 11788
www.barronseduc.com

Library of Congress Control Number: 2017952104

ISBN: 978-1-4380-1116-5

Date of Manufacture: November 2017
Manufactured by: Leo Paper Group, Heshan, China

Printed in China
9 8 7 6 5 4 3 2 1

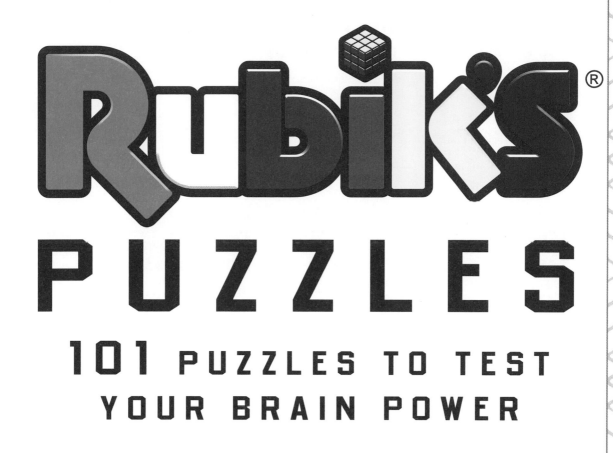

PUZZLES

101 PUZZLES TO TEST YOUR BRAIN POWER

CONTENTS

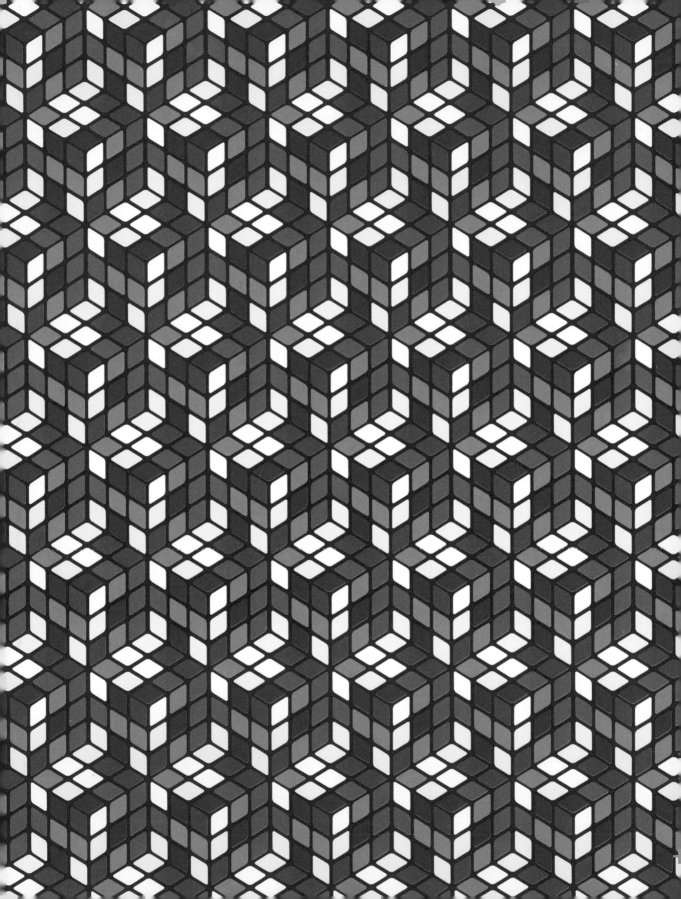

INTRODUCTION

Almost everyone knows Rubik's Cube. That's not an exaggeration—the Cube is familiar to ninety-eight percent of the world. It's an incredible feat, so it's no surprise that the Cube is the world's best-selling toy ever, and it's still the fastest-selling puzzle.

By the mid 1980s, just a few years after its launch, at least a fifth of the people on Earth had played with one. Even if that number has dipped slightly since those heady days, Rubik's Cube is hardly old news. Sales have increased sixty-one percent over the last few years to over one hundred million in 2015 alone.

Professor Ernö Rubik was working at the Academy of Applied Arts and Crafts in Budapest when he created his Cube in 1974. He was attempting to find a solution to the issue of having a structure movable in all three dimensions without it falling to pieces. Once he succeeded, he scrambled the device and realized it was going to be very hard to get it back into its original alignment. He patented his new toy in 1975, and it was released in Budapest in 1977. A fellow Hungarian, Tibor Laczi, took the Cube to the Nuremberg Toy Fair—still the world's largest—in 1979. At the fair, the British businessman Tom Kremer realized the potential, and brokered a deal with Ideal Toys, an American toy and game firm.

Ideal renamed the Cube from Professor Rubik's modest pick of "Magic Cube" to a more punchy "Rubik's Cube," and the first Rubik's Cubes shipped out in May of 1980. The Cube immediately won lots and lots of awards, hit the public consciousness, and

exploded. In that first craze, two hundred million Cubes were sold between 1980 and 1983. The first speed-solving championships took place in Munich in 1981. The 2017 championships took place in Paris. Between 1982 and 2016, the world record time to solve a thoroughly scrambled Cube dropped from 19 seconds to just 4.73 seconds (by Feliks Zemdegs of Amsterdam).

Along with the fame of the Cube came lots of books on how to solve it, including one by world-leading puzzle and recreational mathematics professor David Singmaster. This book is something different—a set of carefully designed logic and spatial awareness puzzles that will test your brain rather than your manual dexterity. They do get more and more challenging, in general, as you progress through the book. However, you don't need to be a Cube expert to enjoy these puzzles, or even to have actually ever picked one up. All you require is some determination and a bit of clear thinking.

Have fun!
Tim Dedopulos

Each puzzle has been rated at the following difficulty levels:

RUBIK'S CHALLENGE LEVEL
1 2 3 4 5 6 7 8 9 10

Levels 1-3: **BEGINNER** Entry level puzzles for beginners
Levels 4-6: **MEDIUM** difficulty for puzzle enthusiasts
Levels 7-10: **DIFFICULT** The hardest level for accomplished puzzle and games fans

1

1 MAZE

Moving horizontally or vertically in the color sequence shown in the top bar, can you find the path leading from the black square on the left to the black square on the right?

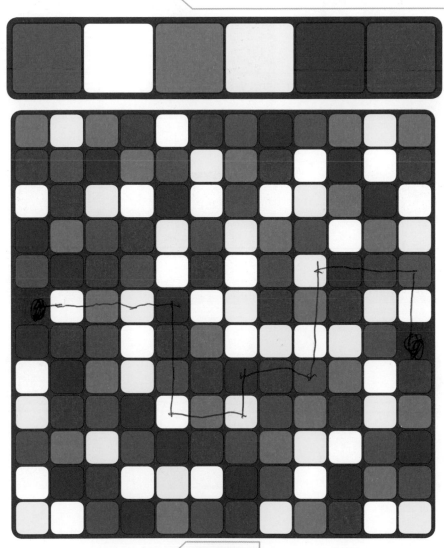

ANSWER SEE PAGE 110

ODD ONE OUT

Which of the squares below is the odd one out?

A

B

C

D

E

F

G

H

I

ANSWER SEE PAGE 110

3

PAIRS

The shape below is composed of 21 paired-square tiles, all pressed together. Each color is paired with every color exactly once, so one pair is white and white, the next is white and yellow, and so on, like dominoes. Can you figure out where the pairs are?

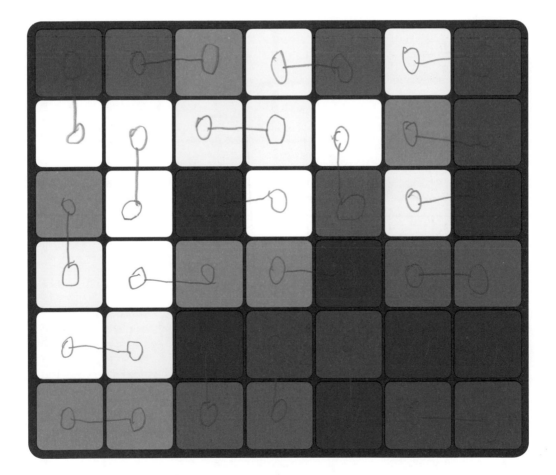

ANSWER SEE PAGE 110

4

LINK

Join each same-colored pair of highlighted cells below with a path of the same color. Paths may not cross, nor may they double back to ever form a square of four cells of the same color. The correct solution uses every cell in the grid exactly once. Can you complete the grid?

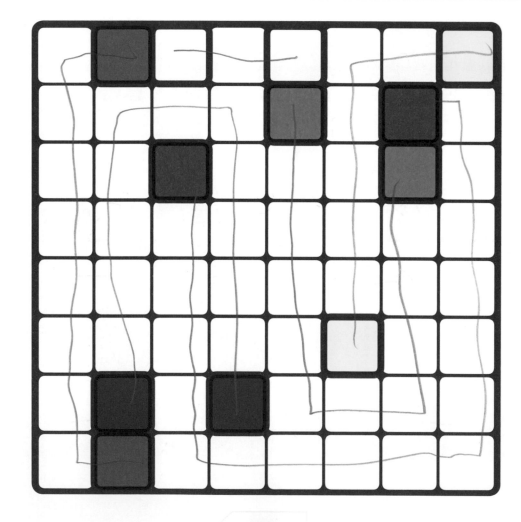

ANSWER SEE PAGE 111

5

CUBE MAP

Which of the Cubes 1-6 cannot be made from the Cube template above?

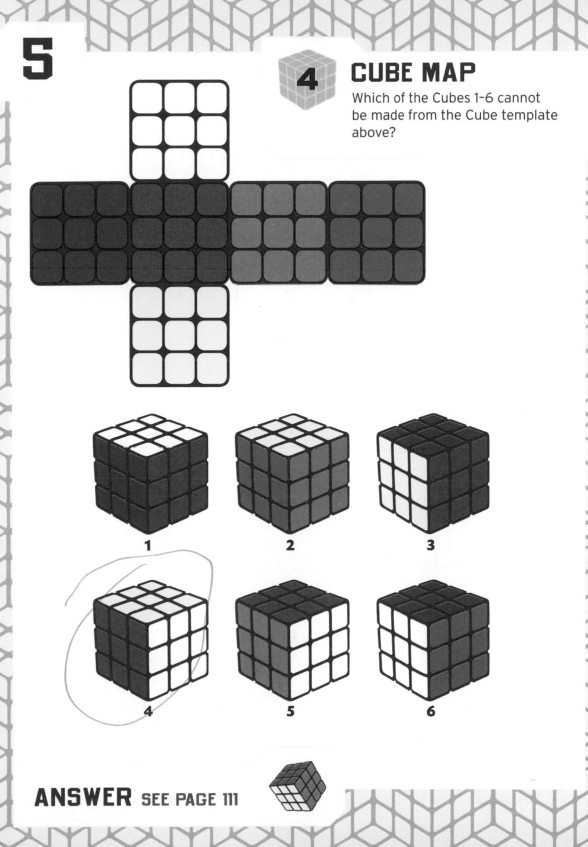

1

2

3

4

5

6

13

ANSWER SEE PAGE 111

BLACK OUT

Black out certain squares in the grid so that no color occurs more than once in each row and column. All remaining colored squares must form a group of two or more, with each square touching another colored square either horizontally or vertically. Black squares must not touch other black squares horizontally or vertically. Can you complete the grid?

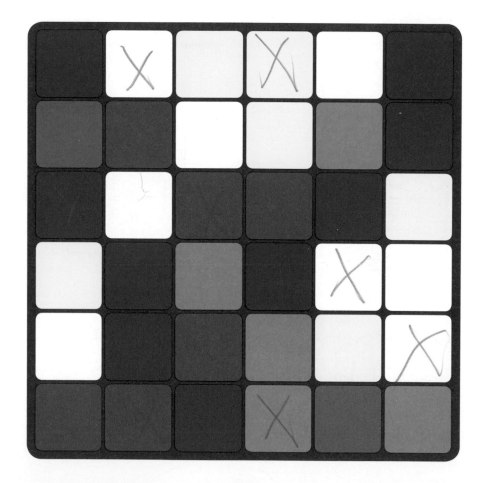

ANSWER SEE PAGE 111

ISLANDS

The grid below is divided into a number of groups composed of vertically and/or horizontally connected tiles. The numbers and colors on certain tiles below indicate the size of the group that tile is part of. No two groups of the same size touch each other. The whole grid is used, but not all groups are indicated below. Can you complete the grid?

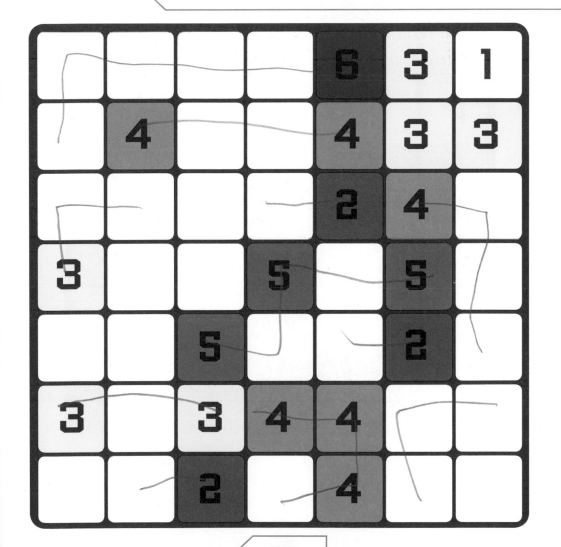

ANSWER SEE PAGE 112

ABSTRACTION

The diagram below follows a specific logic. What letter should replace the question mark?

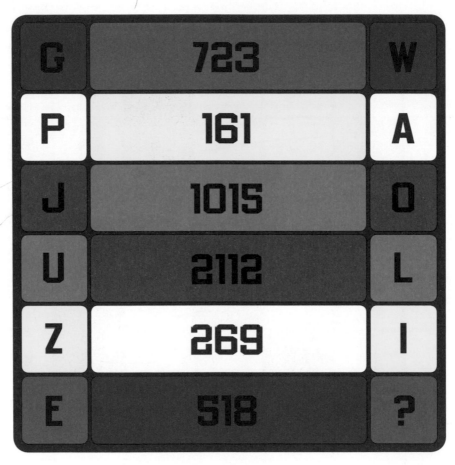

G	723	W
P	161	A
J	1015	O
U	2112	L
Z	269	I
E	518	?

?=R

ANSWER SEE PAGE 112

9

6

EXPLODED

The pieces below have been exploded from a 5x5 square, where each row across is the same as its equivalent column down (1st column = 1st row, etc.). Can you reassemble it?

17

ANSWER SEE PAGE 112

NEXT UP

Which square A-D continues the sequence?

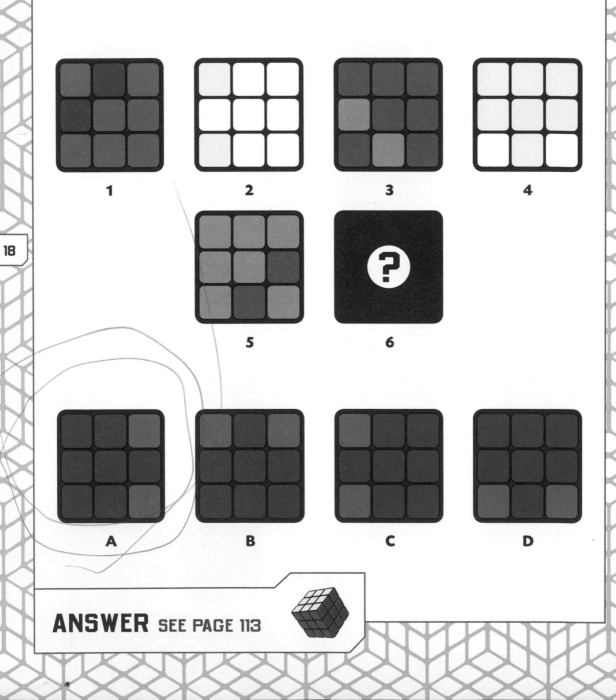

1

2

3

4

5

6

A

B

C

D

ANSWER SEE PAGE 113

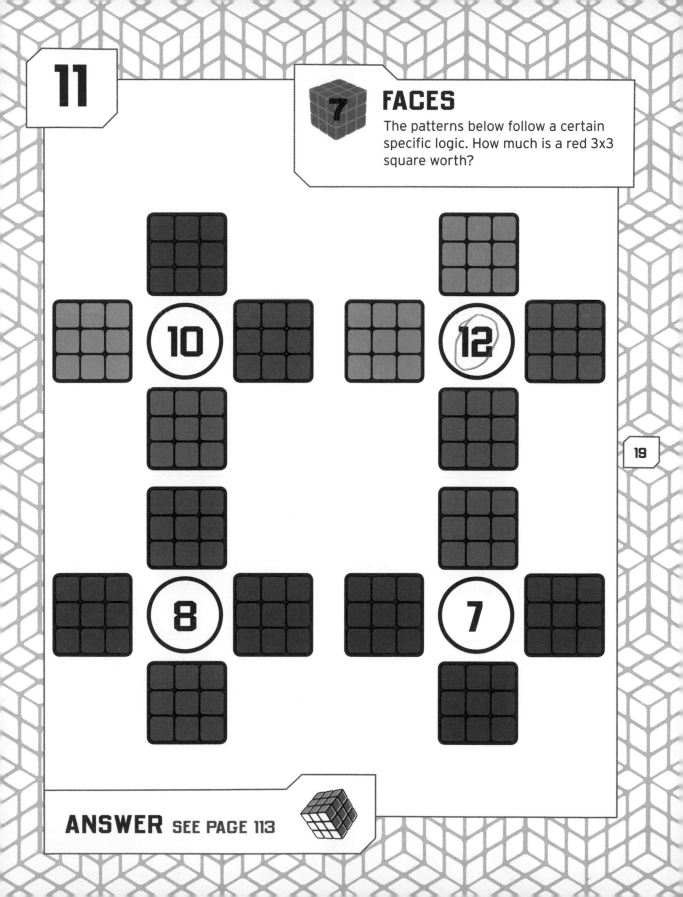

FACES

The patterns below follow a certain specific logic. How much is a red 3x3 square worth?

ANSWER SEE PAGE 113

12

7 FACE SEQUENCE

Which of the four squares below completes the pattern?

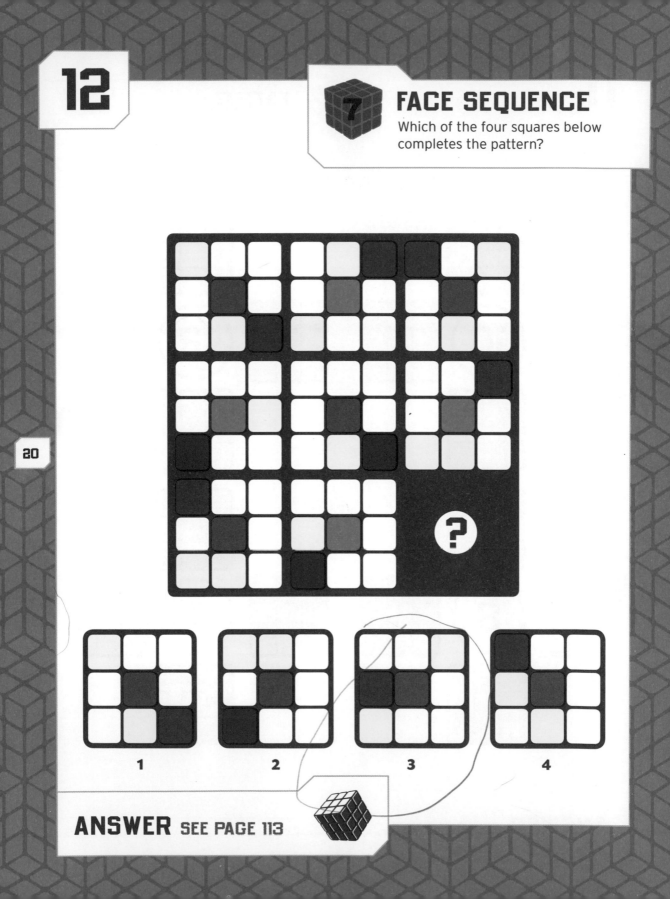

1   2   3   4

ANSWER SEE PAGE 113

13

4 TWO-TONE

In the grid below, each row and column contains exactly 4 squares of each of the two colors. No more than two squares of the same color can touch in a horizontal or vertical line. Can you complete the grid?

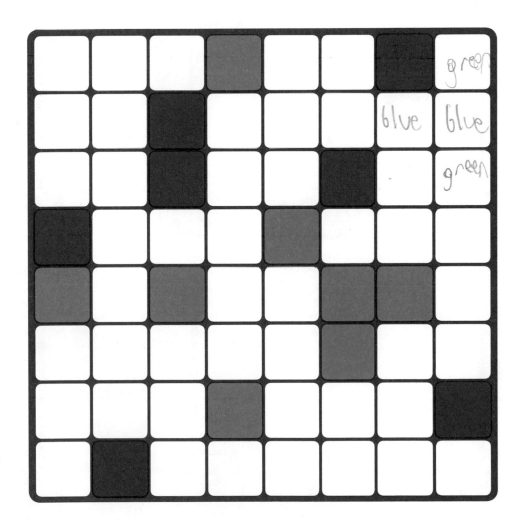

ANSWER SEE PAGE 114

MATHEMATICAL

The squares below follow a certain consistent logic. What value should replace the question mark?

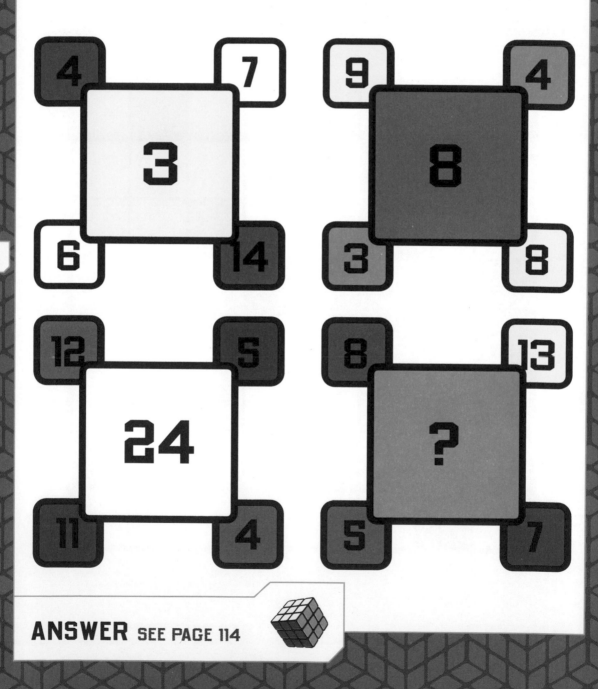

ANSWER SEE PAGE 114

2 HEXAGONAL

Which of the tile patterns A-F cannot be found in the hexagonal grid?

A

B

C

D

E

F

ANSWER SEE PAGE 114

16

CASCADE

In the triangle, each cell is the total of the two cells immediately below it. Can you place the numbers from the list below to correctly complete the triangle?

| 13 | 20 | 137 | 15 | -10 | 18 |

| 21 | 43 | 56 | 295 | 23 | 39 | 81 |

| -6 | 77 | 131 | 289 | 54 | 584 | 158 |

ANSWER SEE PAGE 115

7 TOTALS
What is the value of a red square?

11
19
18
15
14

14 18 13 13 19

ANSWER SEE PAGE 115

TWO-TONE

In the grid below, each row and column contains exactly 4 squares of each of the two colors. No more than two squares of the same color can touch in a horizontal or vertical line. Can you complete the grid?

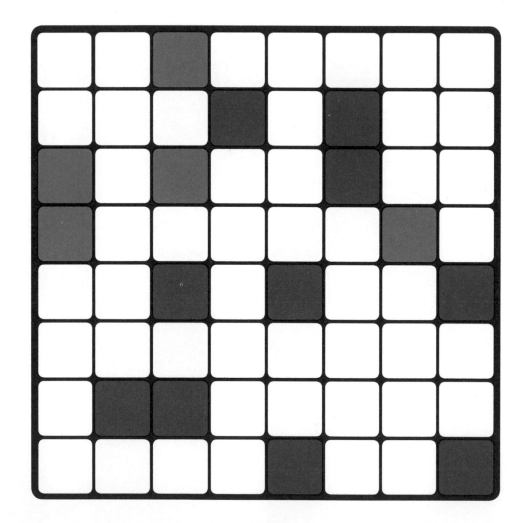

ANSWER SEE PAGE 115

LINK

Join each same-colored pair of highlighted cells below with a path of the same color. Paths may not cross, nor may they double back to ever form a square of four cells of the same color. The correct solution uses every cell in the grid exactly once. Can you complete the grid?

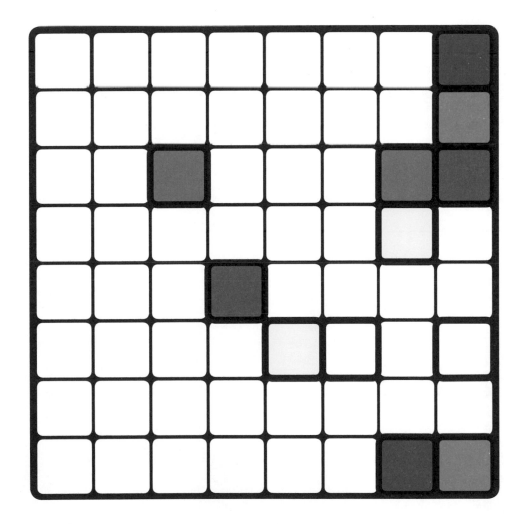

ANSWER SEE PAGE 116

MATHEMATICAL

8

The squares below follow a certain consistent logic. What value should replace the question mark?

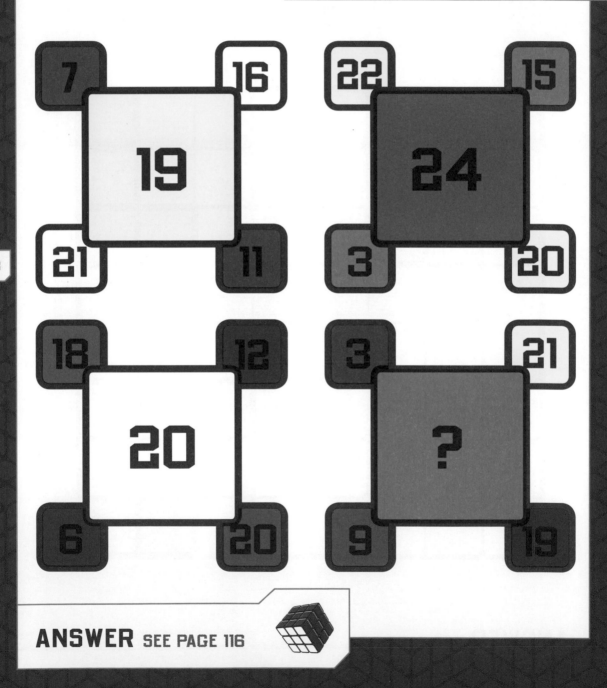

7 16	22 15
19	**24**
21 11	3 20
18 12	3 21
20	**?**
6 20	9 19

ANSWER SEE PAGE 116

21

ISLANDS

The grid below is divided into a number of groups composed of vertically and/or horizontally connected tiles. The numbers and colors on certain tiles below indicate the size of the group that tile is part of. No two groups of the same size touch each other. The whole grid is used, but not all groups are indicated below. Can you complete the grid?

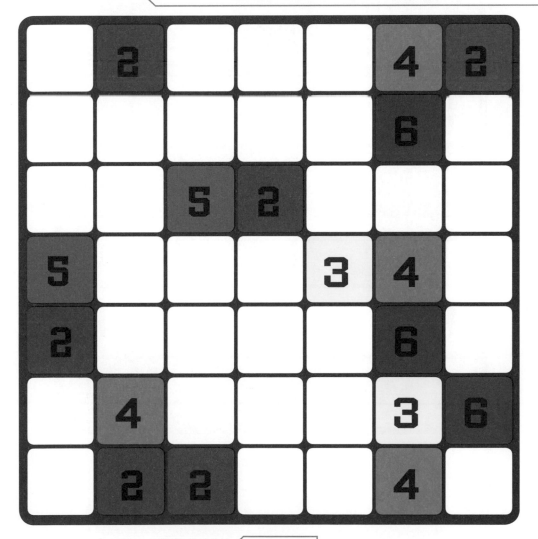

ANSWER SEE PAGE 116

22

 8

ABSTRACTION

The diagram below follows a specific logic. What letter should replace the question mark?

30

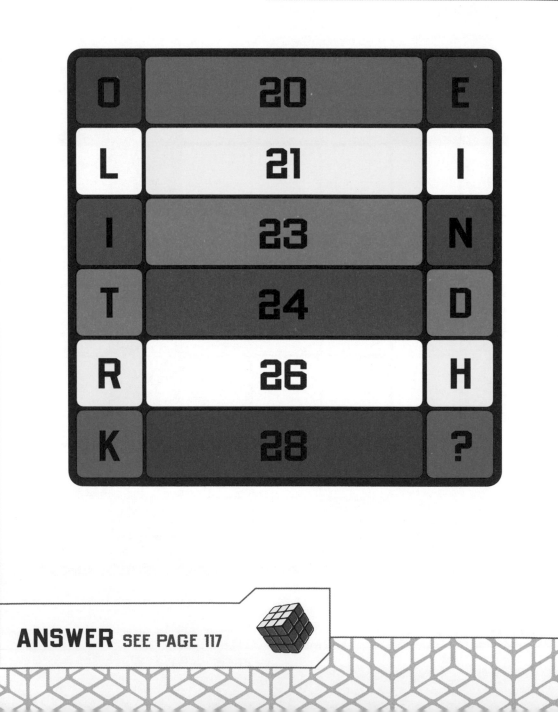

O	20	E
L	21	I
I	23	N
T	24	D
R	26	H
K	28	?

ANSWER SEE PAGE 117

ODD ONE OUT

Which of the squares below is the odd one out?

A

B

C

D

E

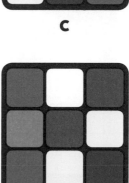

F

G

H

I

ANSWER SEE PAGE 117

4 BLACK OUT

Black out certain squares in the grid so that no color occurs more than once in each row and column. All remaining colored squares must form a group of two or more, with each square touching another colored square either horizontally or vertically. Black squares must not touch other black squares horizontally or vertically. Can you complete the grid?

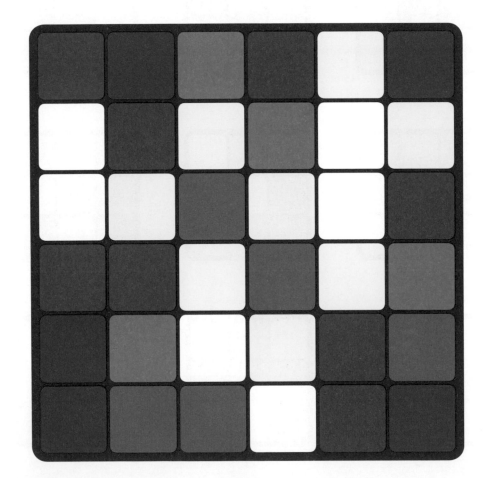

ANSWER SEE PAGE 117

NEXT UP

Which square A–D continues the sequence?

1

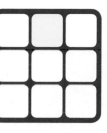

2

3

4

5

6

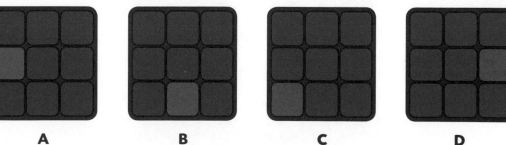

A   **B**   **C**   **D**

ANSWER SEE PAGE 118

CASCADE

In the triangle, each cell is the total of the two cells immediately below it. Can you place the numbers from the list below to correctly complete the triangle?

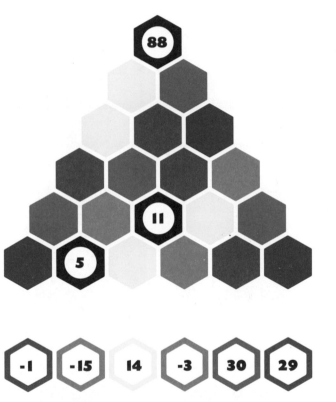

27

PAIRS

The shape below is composed of 21 paired-square tiles, all pressed together. Each color is paired with every color exactly once, so one pair is white and white, the next is white and yellow, and so on, like dominoes. Can you figure out where the pairs are?

ANSWER SEE PAGE 118

6 EXPLODED

The pieces below have been exploded from a 5x5 square, where each row across is the same as its equivalent column down (1st column = 1st row, etc.). Can you reassemble it?

ANSWER SEE PAGE 119

FACES

The patterns below follow a certain specific logic. How much is a red 3x3 square worth?

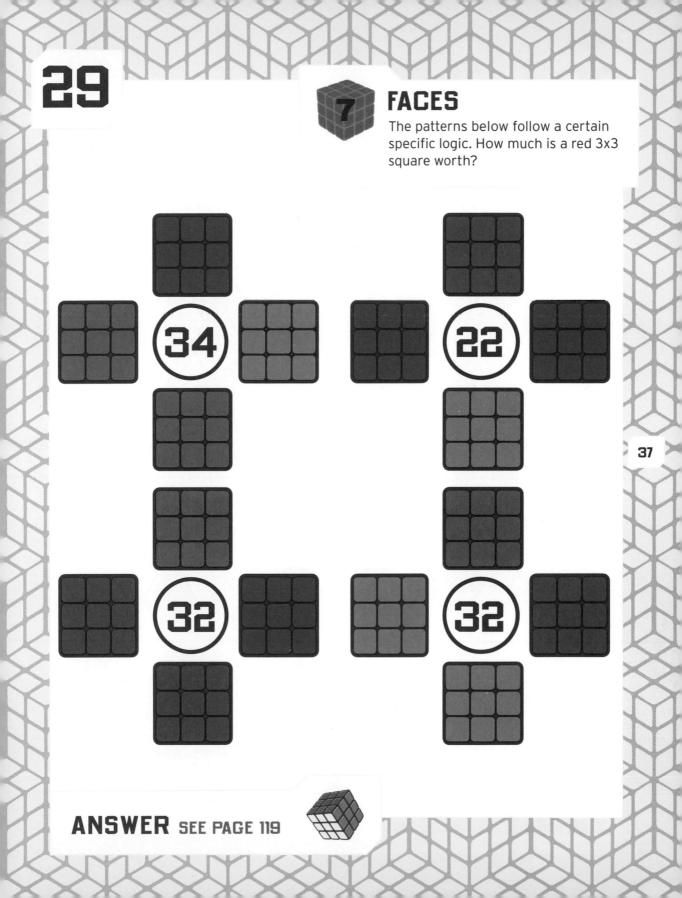

ANSWER SEE PAGE 119

2 HEXAGONAL

Which of the tile patterns A-F cannot be found in the hexagonal grid?

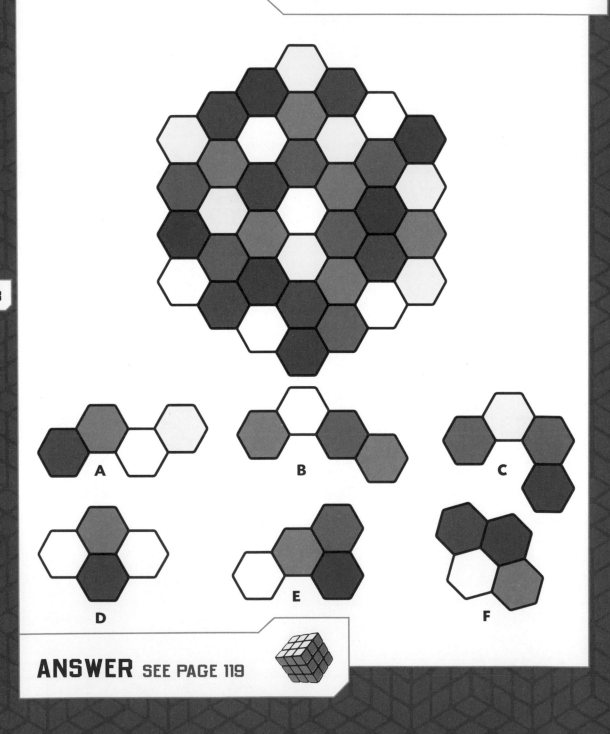

A

B

C

D

E

F

ANSWER SEE PAGE 119

MAZE

Moving horizontally or vertically in the color sequence shown in the top bar, can you find the path leading from the black square on the left to the black square on the right?

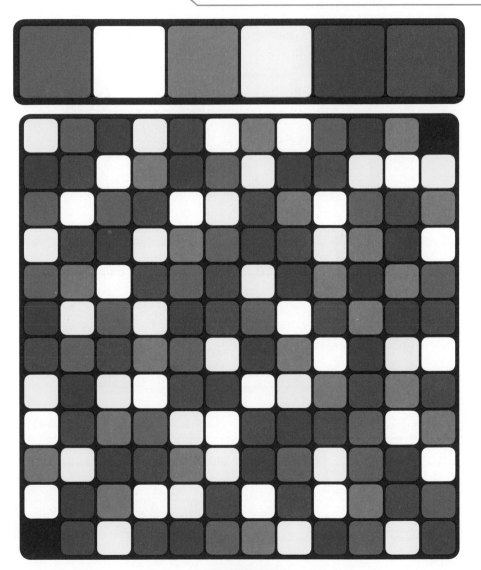

ANSWER SEE PAGE 120

32

FACE SEQUENCE

Which of the four squares below completes the pattern?

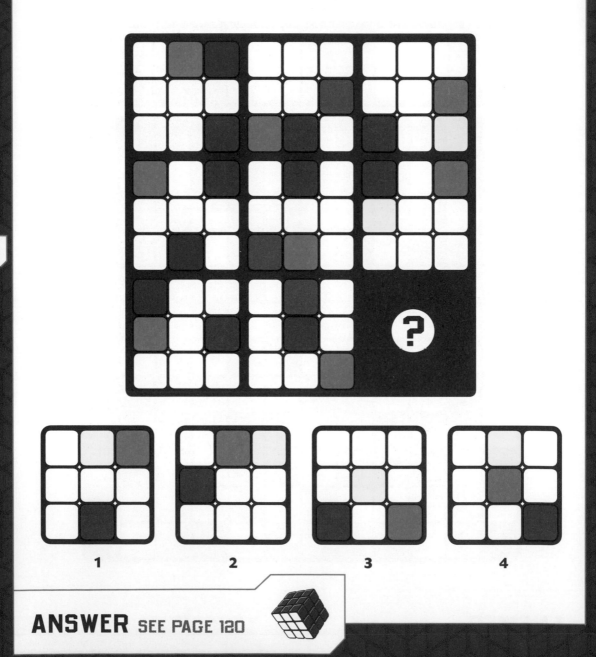

1

2

3

4

ANSWER SEE PAGE 120

33

TOTALS
What is the value of a red square?

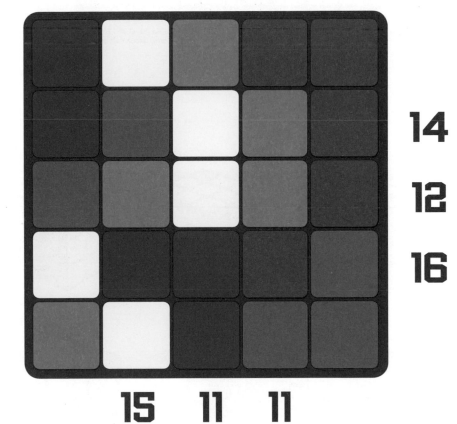

14

12

16

15 11 11

ANSWER SEE PAGE 120

34

CUBE MAP

Which of the Cubes 1-6 cannot be made from the Cube template above?

1

2

3

4

5

6

42

ANSWER SEE PAGE 121

35

7 PAIRS

The shape below is composed of 21 paired-square tiles, all pressed together. Each color is paired with every color exactly once, so one pair is white and white, the next is white and yellow, and so on, like dominoes. Can you figure out where the pairs are?

ANSWER SEE PAGE 121

FACES

The patterns below follow a certain specific logic. How much is a red 3x3 square worth?

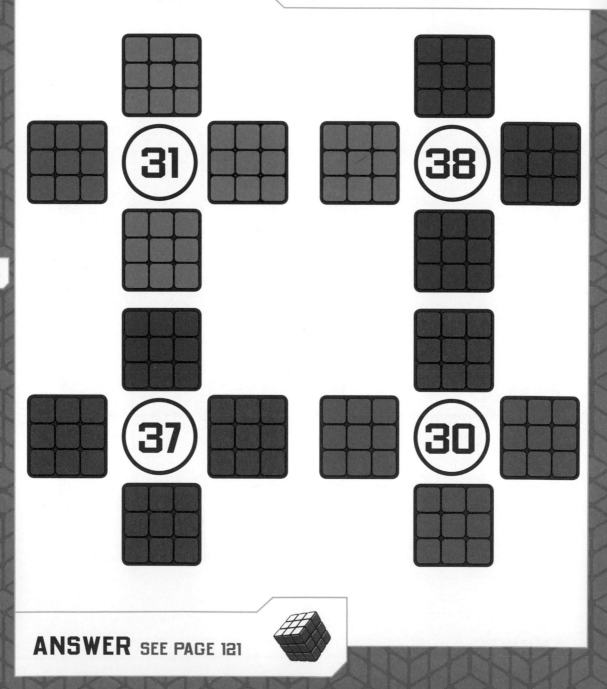

ANSWER SEE PAGE 121

EXPLODED

The pieces below have been exploded from a 5x5 square, where each row across is the same as its equivalent column down (1st column = 1st row, etc.). Can you reassemble it?

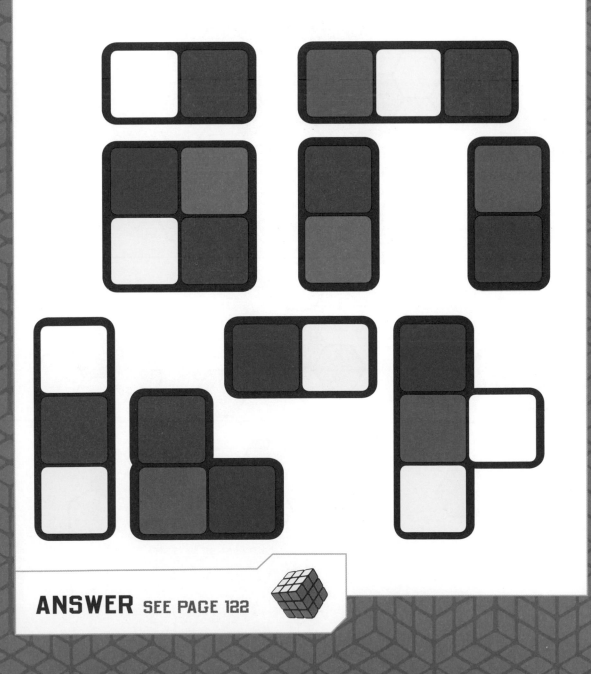

ANSWER SEE PAGE 122

HEXAGONAL

Which of the tile patterns A-F cannot be found in the hexagonal grid?

A

B

C

D

E

F

ANSWER SEE PAGE 122

TOTALS
What is the value of a red square?

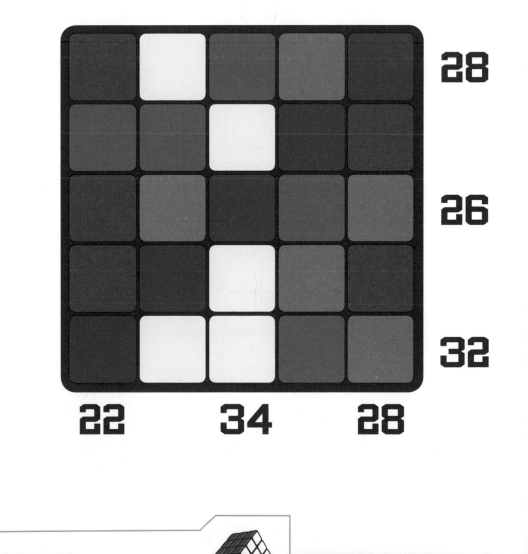

28

26

32

22   34   28

ANSWER SEE PAGE 122

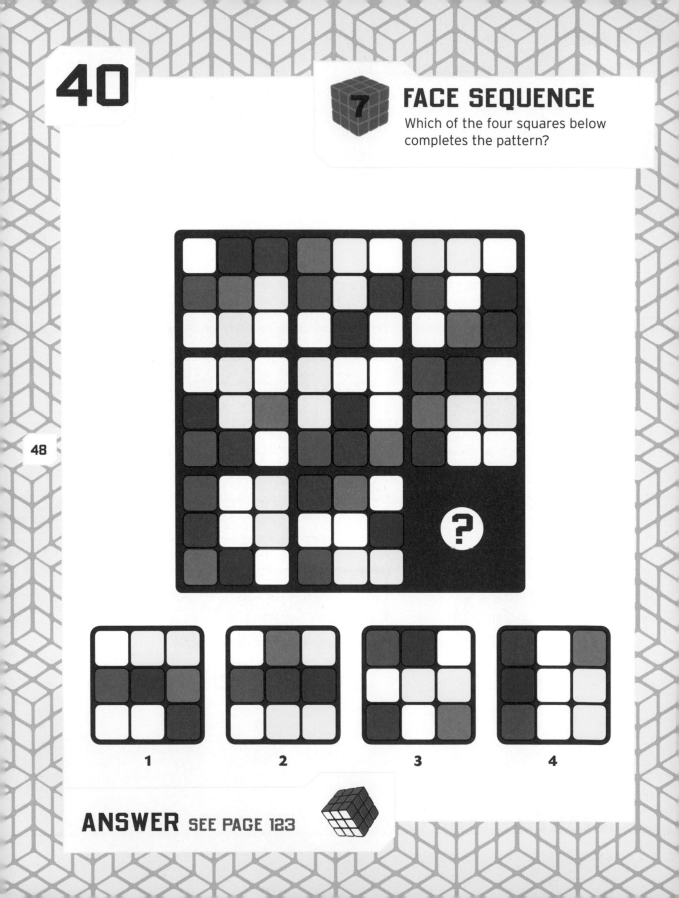

40

7 FACE SEQUENCE
Which of the four squares below completes the pattern?

48

1   2   3   4

ANSWER SEE PAGE 123

NEXT UP

Which square A-D continues the sequence?

1

2

3

4

5

6

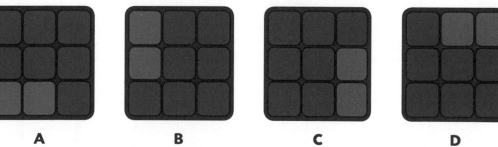

A　　**B**　　**C**　　**D**

ANSWER SEE PAGE 123

42

 ## LINK

Join each same-colored pair of highlighted cells below with a path of the same color. Paths may not cross, nor may they double back to ever form a square of four cells of the same color. The correct solution uses every cell in the grid exactly once. Can you complete the grid?

50

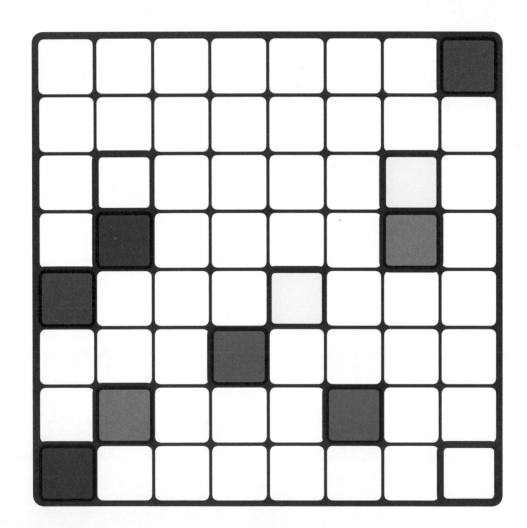

ANSWER SEE PAGE 123

ABSTRACTION

The diagram below follows a specific logic. What letter should replace the question mark?

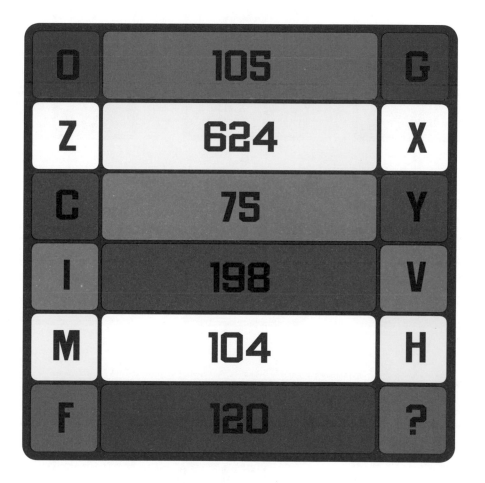

O	105	G
Z	624	X
C	75	Y
I	198	V
M	104	H
F	120	?

ANSWER SEE PAGE 124

ODD ONE OUT

Which of the squares below is the odd one out?

A

B

C

D

E

F

G

H

I

ANSWER SEE PAGE 124

ISLANDS

The grid below is divided into a number of groups composed of vertically and/or horizontally connected tiles. The numbers and colors on certain tiles below indicate the size of the group that tile is part of. No two groups of the same size touch each other. The whole grid is used, but not all groups are indicated below. Can you complete the grid?

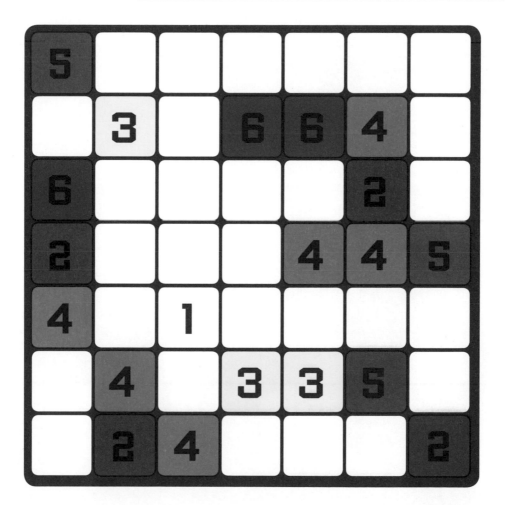

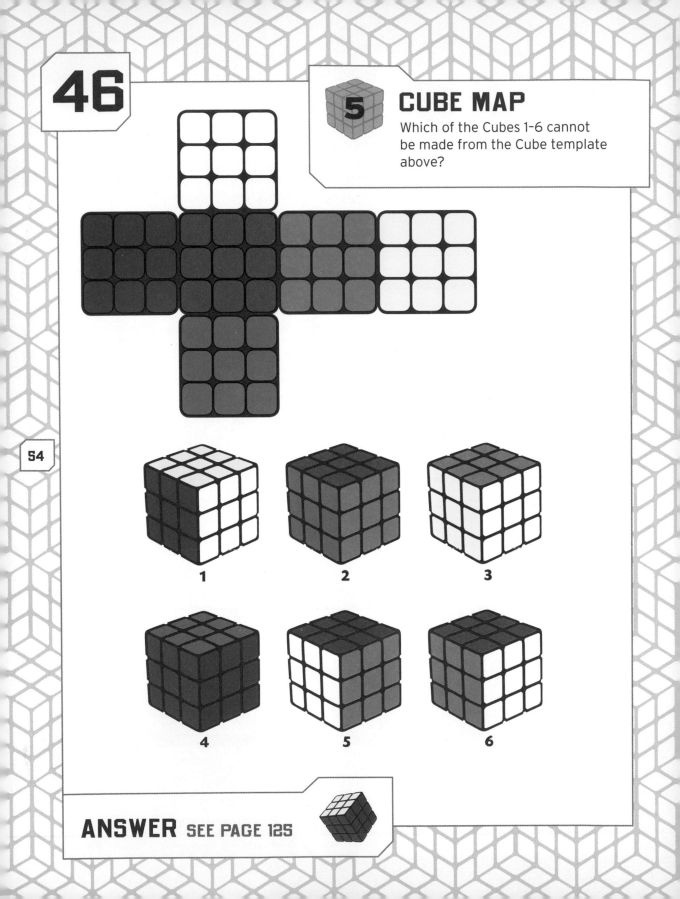

5 CUBE MAP

Which of the Cubes 1-6 cannot be made from the Cube template above?

1

2

3

4

5

6

ANSWER SEE PAGE 125

TWO-TONE

In the grid below, each row and column contains exactly 4 squares of each of the two colors. No more than two squares of the same color can touch in a horizontal or vertical line. Can you complete the grid?

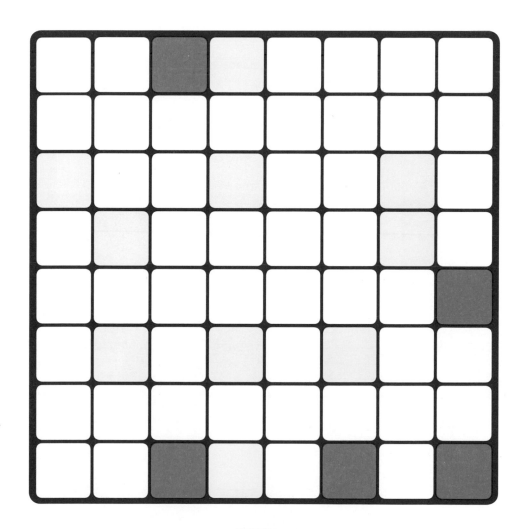

ANSWER SEE PAGE 125

BLACK OUT

Black out certain squares in the grid so that no color occurs more than once in each row and column. All remaining colored squares must form a group of two or more, with each square touching another colored square either horizontally or vertically. Black squares must not touch other black squares horizontally or vertically. Can you complete the grid?

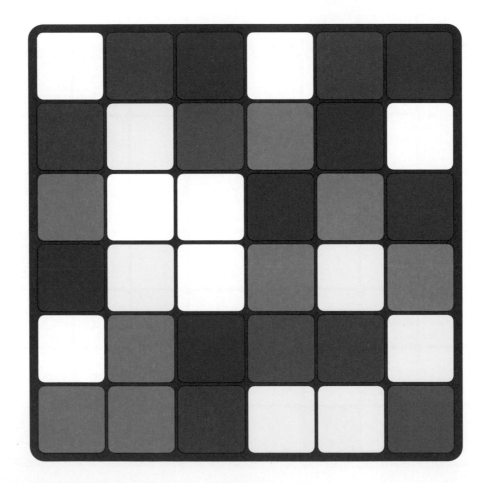

ANSWER SEE PAGE 125

49

CASCADE

In the triangle, each cell is the total of the two cells immediately below it. Can you place the numbers from the list below to correctly complete the triangle?

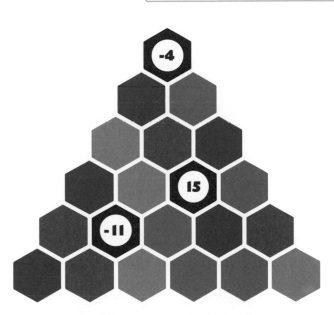

-4

15

-11

| -1 | -4 | 25 | 33 | -31 | -19 |

| 7 | -7 | 8 | -6 | -21 | -23 |

| 9 | -10 | 18 | 16 | 27 | -25 |

ANSWER SEE PAGE 126

MATHEMATICAL

The squares below follow a certain consistent logic. What value should replace the question mark?

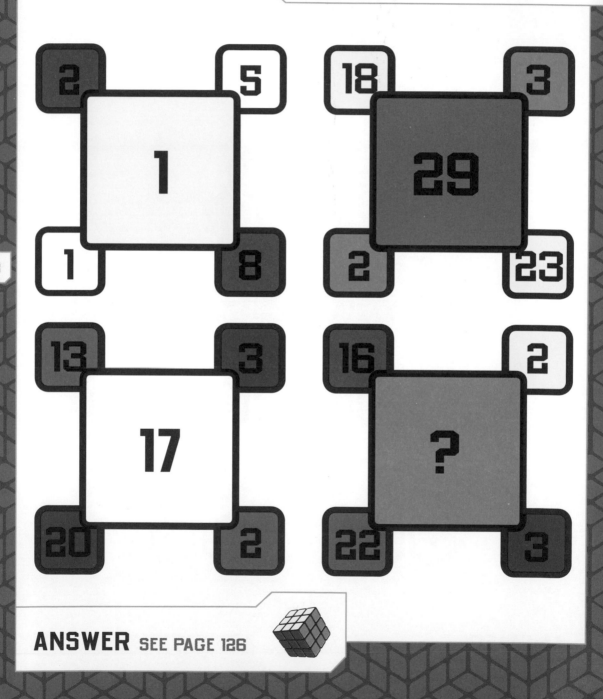

ANSWER SEE PAGE 126

1 MAZE

Moving horizontally or vertically in the color sequence shown in the top bar, can you find the path leading from the black square on the left to the black square on the right?

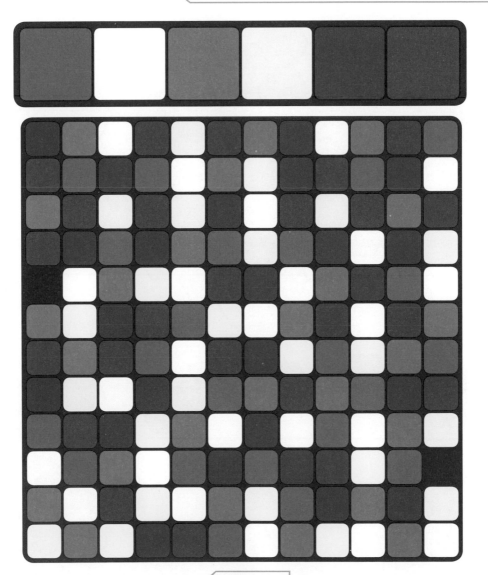

ANSWER SEE PAGE 126

2 HEXAGONAL
Which of the tile patterns A–F cannot be found in the hexagonal grid?

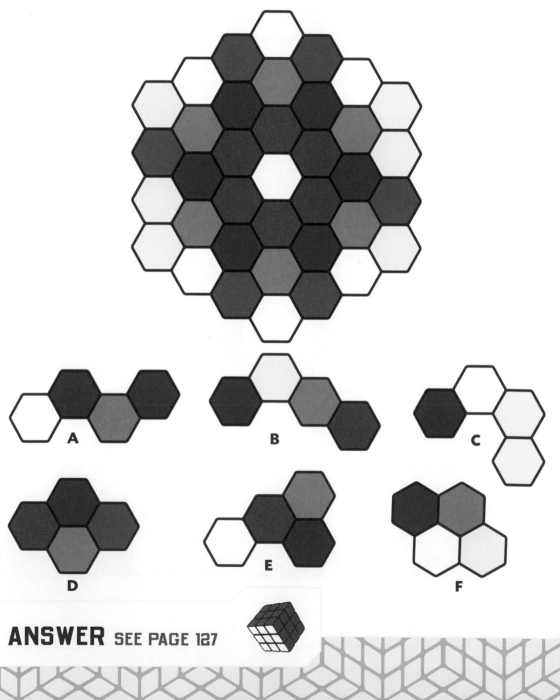

A

B

C

D

E

F

ANSWER SEE PAGE 127

FACE SEQUENCE
Which of the four squares below completes the pattern?

1 **2** **3** **4**

ANSWER SEE PAGE 127

TWO-TONE

In the grid below, each row and column contains exactly 4 squares of each of the two colors. No more than two squares of the same color can touch in a horizontal or vertical line. Can you complete the grid?

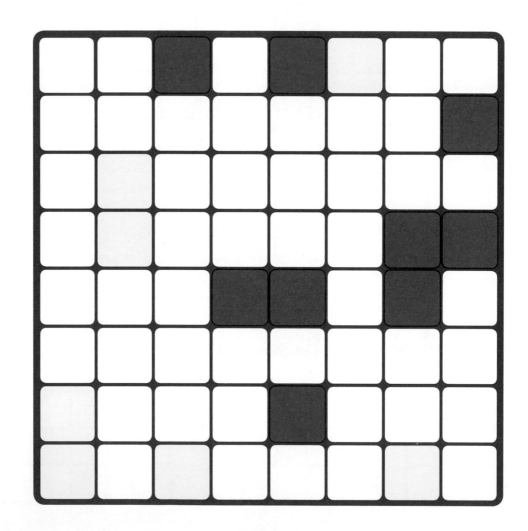

ANSWER SEE PAGE 127

TOTALS
What is the value of a red square?

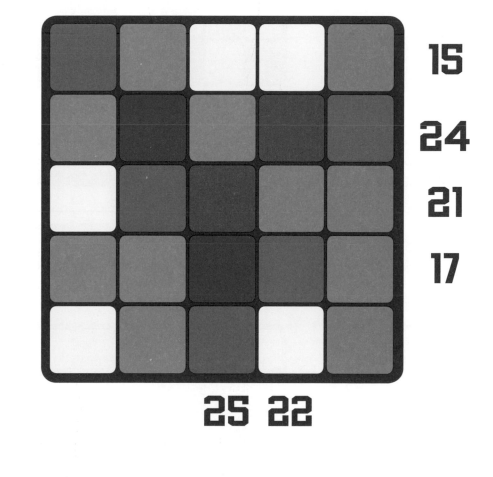

15

24

21

17

25 22

ANSWER SEE PAGE 128

ODD ONE OUT

Which of the squares below is the odd one out?

A

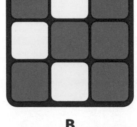

B

C

D

E

F

G

H

I

ANSWER SEE PAGE 128

FACES

The patterns below follow a certain specific logic. How much is a red 3x3 square worth?

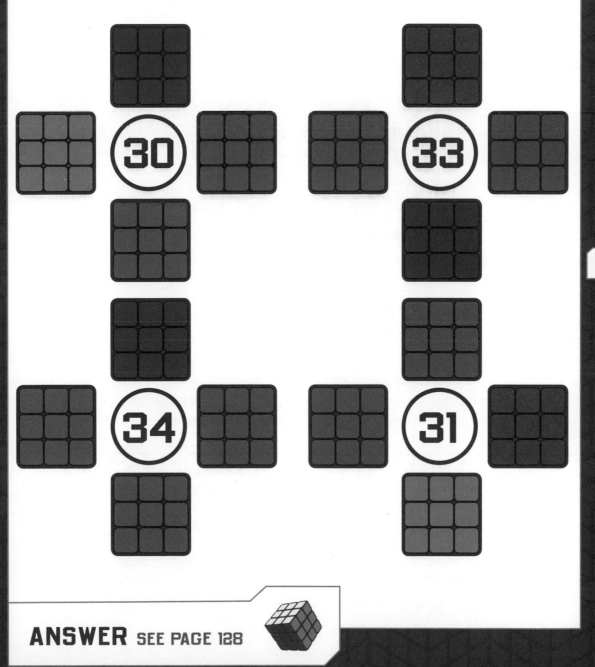

ANSWER SEE PAGE 128

CASCADE

In the triangle, each cell is the total of the two cells immediately below it. Can you place the numbers from the list below to correctly complete the triangle?

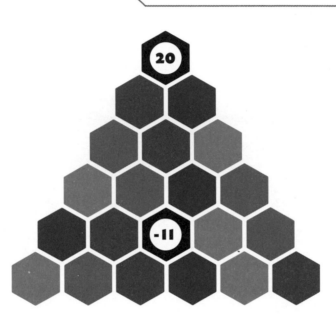

ANSWER SEE PAGE 129

4 BLACK OUT

Black out certain squares in the grid so that no color occurs more than once in each row and column. All remaining colored squares must form a group of two or more, with each square touching another colored square either horizontally or vertically. Black squares must not touch other black squares horizontally or vertically. Can you complete the grid?

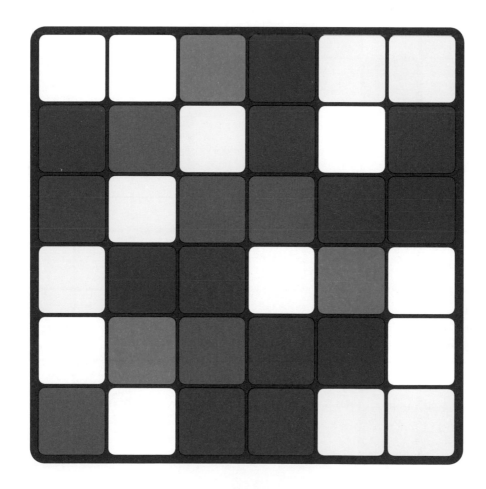

ANSWER SEE PAGE 129

LINK

Join each same-colored pair of highlighted cells below with a path of the same color. Paths may not cross, nor may they double back to ever form a square of four cells of the same color. The correct solution uses every cell in the grid exactly once. Can you complete the grid?

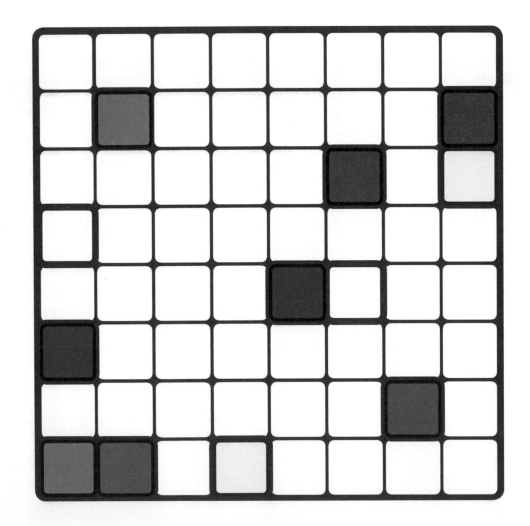

ANSWER SEE PAGE 129

1 MAZE

Moving horizontally or vertically in the color sequence shown in the top bar, can you find the path leading from the black square on the left to the black square on the right?

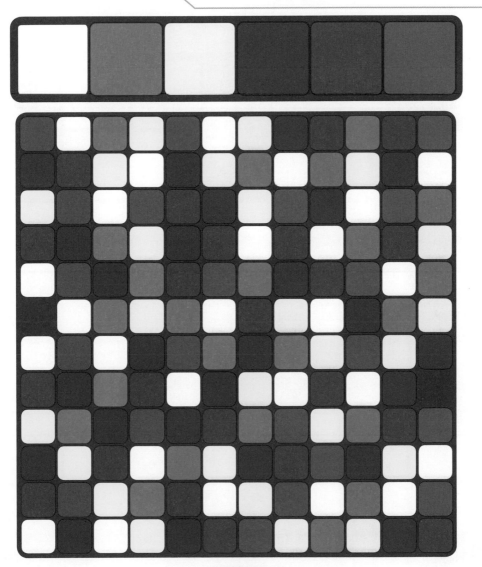

ANSWER SEE PAGE 130

62

ISLANDS

The grid below is divided into a number of groups composed of vertically and/or horizontally connected tiles. The numbers and colors on certain tiles below indicate the size of the group that tile is part of. No two groups of the same size touch each other. The whole grid is used, but not all groups are indicated below. Can you complete the grid?

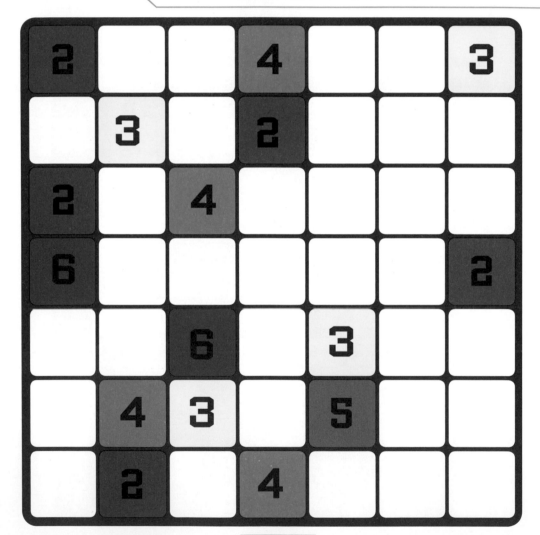

ANSWER SEE PAGE 130

NEXT UP

Which square A–D continues the sequence?

1

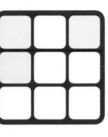

2

3

4

5

6

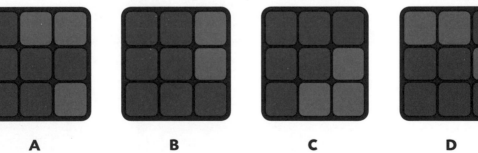

A

B

C

D

ANSWER SEE PAGE 130

64

EXPLODED

The pieces below have been exploded from a 5x5 square, where each row across is the same as its equivalent column down (1st column = 1st row, etc.). Can you reassemble it?

72

ANSWER SEE PAGE 131

PAIRS

The shape below is composed of 21 paired-square tiles, all pressed together. Each color is paired with every color exactly once, so one pair is white and white, the next is white and yellow, and so on, like dominoes. Can you figure out where the pairs are?

ANSWER SEE PAGE 131

MATHEMATICAL

The squares below follow a certain consistent logic. What value should replace the question mark?

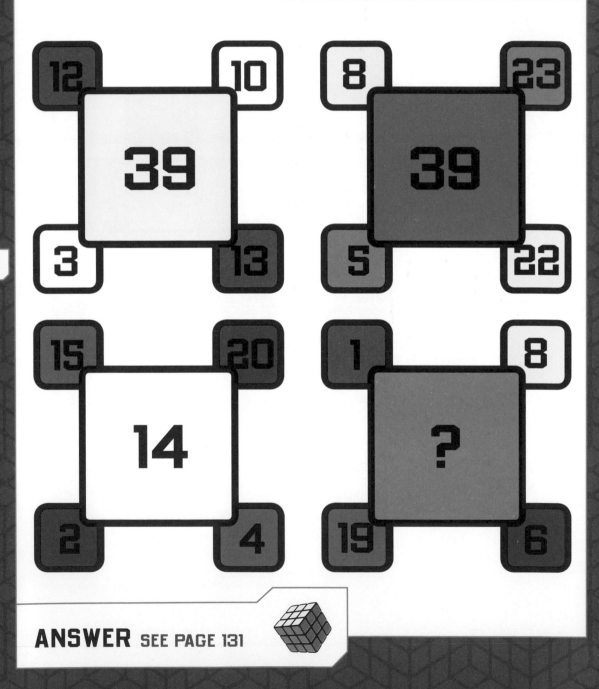

ANSWER SEE PAGE 131

67

ANSWER SEE PAGE 132

5 CUBE MAP

Which of the Cubes 1-6 cannot be made from the Cube template above?

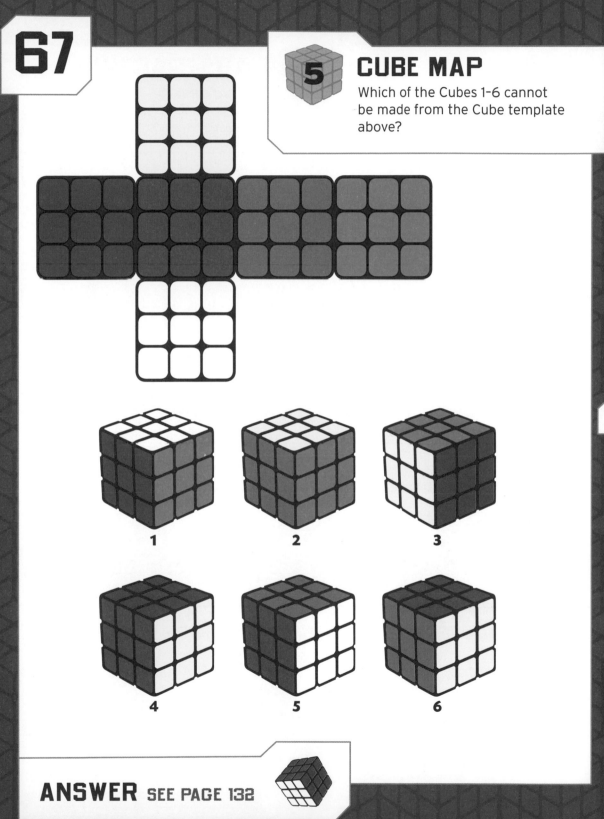

1

2

3

4

5

6

9 ABSTRACTION
The diagram below follows a specific logic. What letter should replace the question mark?

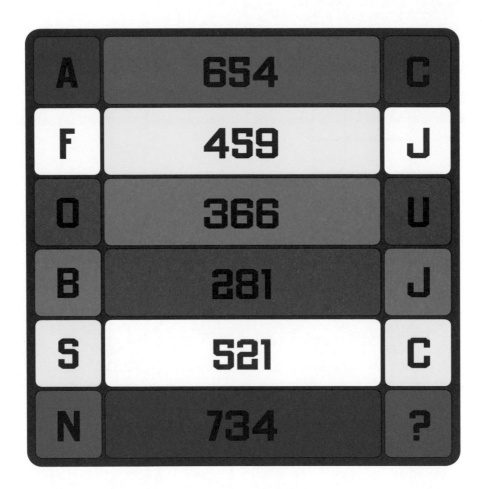

A	654	C
F	459	J
O	366	U
B	281	J
S	521	C
N	734	?

ANSWER SEE PAGE 132

FACE SEQUENCE
Which of the four squares below completes the pattern?

1   2   3   4

ANSWER SEE PAGE 132

1 MAZE

Moving horizontally or vertically in the color sequence shown in the top bar, can you find the path leading from the black square on the left to the black square on the right?

ANSWER SEE PAGE 133

5 CASCADE

In the triangle, each cell is the total of the two cells immediately below it. Can you place the numbers from the list below to correctly complete the triangle?

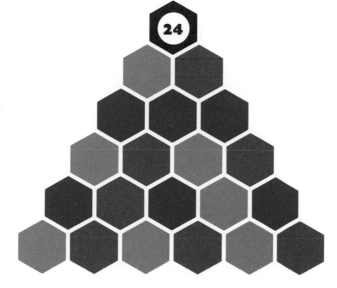

-1 -1 1 4 8 9

1 2 -3 12 15 17 19

-2 3 7 7 -11 -15 -16

ANSWER SEE PAGE 133

TOTALS

What is the value of a red square?

80

29

15

23

17

33

ANSWER SEE PAGE 133

73

MATHEMATICAL

The squares below follow a certain consistent logic. What value should replace the question mark?

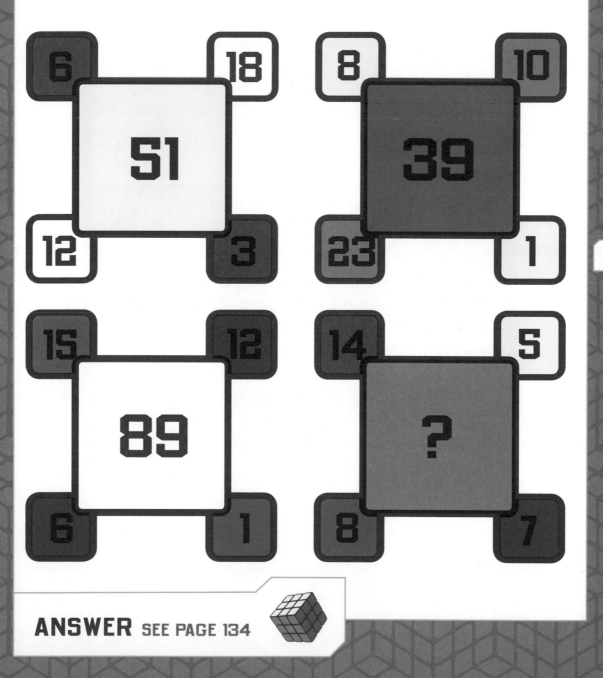

ANSWER SEE PAGE 134

ABSTRACTION

The diagram below follows a specific logic. What letter should replace the question mark?

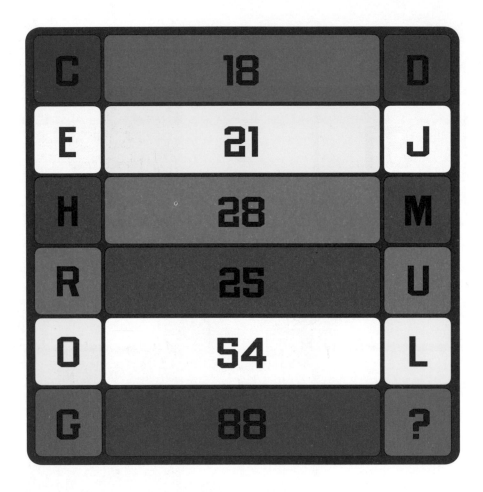

C	18	D
E	21	J
H	28	M
R	25	U
O	54	L
G	88	?

BLACK OUT

Black out certain squares in the grid so that no color occurs more than once in each row and column. All remaining colored squares must form a group of two or more, with each square touching another colored square either horizontally or vertically. Black squares must not touch other black squares horizontally or vertically. Can you complete the grid?

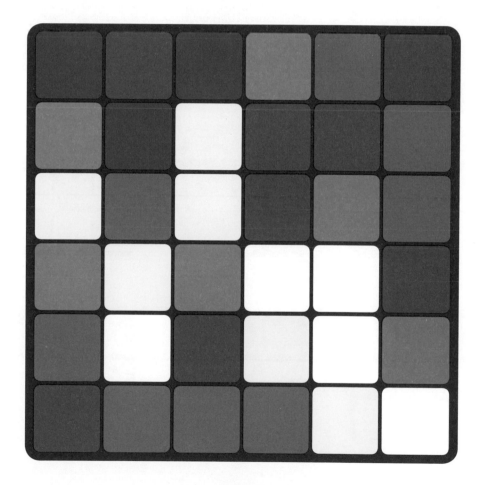

ANSWER SEE PAGE 134

ODD ONE OUT

Which of the squares below is the odd one out?

A

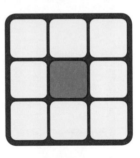

B

C

D

E

F

G

H

I

ANSWER SEE PAGE 135

77

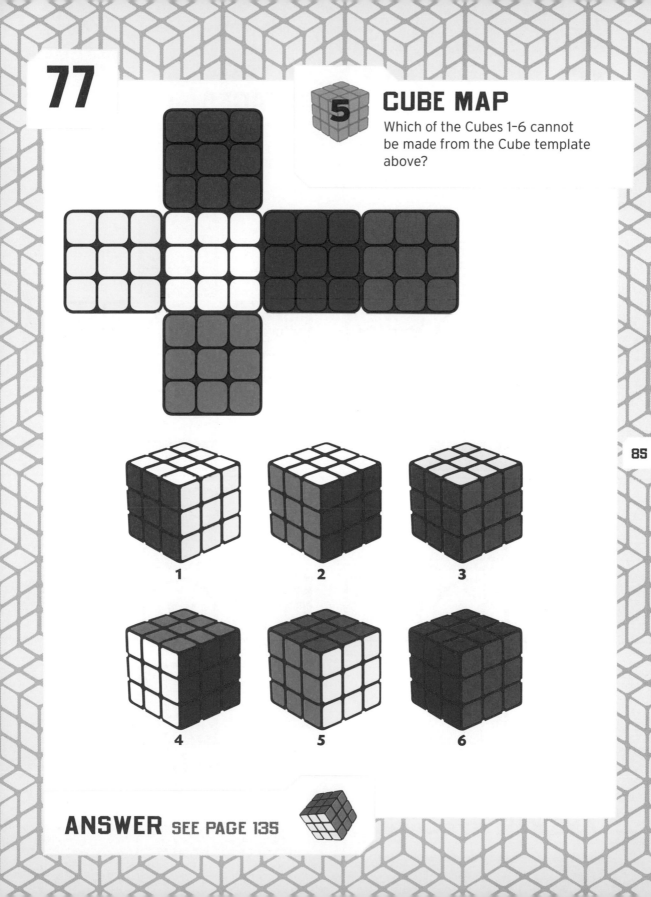

5 CUBE MAP

Which of the Cubes 1-6 cannot be made from the Cube template above?

1

2

3

4

5

6

85

ANSWER SEE PAGE 135

FACES

The patterns below follow a certain specific logic. How much is a red 3x3 square worth?

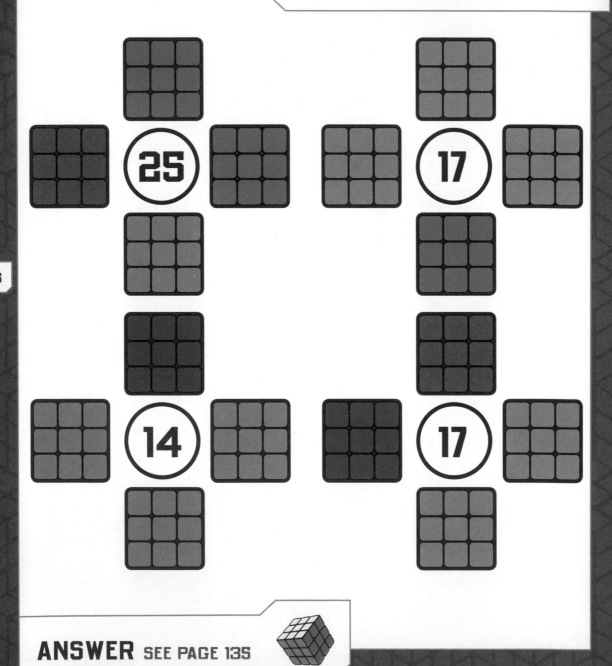

ANSWER SEE PAGE 135

7 **NEXT UP**
Which square A-D continues the sequence?

 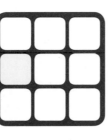  

1   2   3   4

5   6

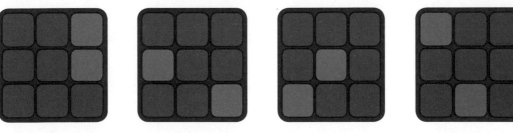

A   B   C   D

ISLANDS

The grid below is divided into a number of groups composed of vertically and/or horizontally connected tiles. The numbers and colors on certain tiles below indicate the size of the group that tile is part of. No two groups of the same size touch each other. The whole grid is used, but not all groups are indicated below. Can you complete the grid?

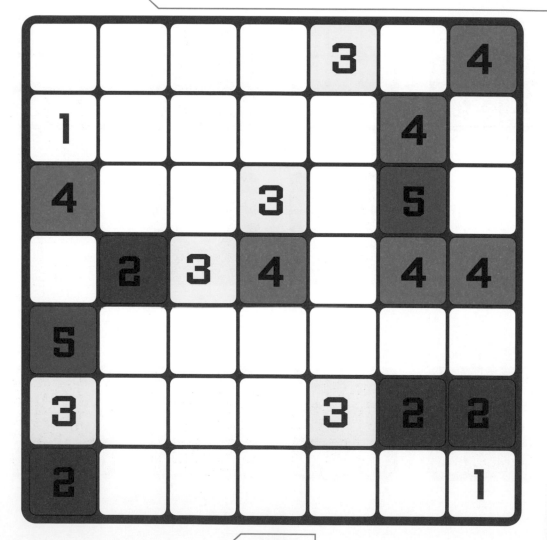

LINK

Join each same-colored pair of highlighted cells below with a path of the same color. Paths may not cross, nor may they double back to ever form a square of four cells of the same color. The correct solution uses every cell in the grid exactly once. Can you complete the grid?

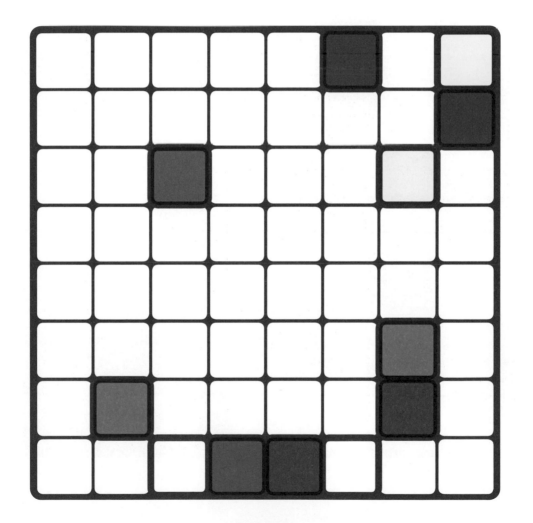

ANSWER SEE PAGE 136

7 PAIRS

The shape below is composed of 21 paired-square tiles, all pressed together. Each color is paired with every color exactly once, so one pair is white and white, the next is white and yellow, and so on, like dominoes. Can you figure out where the pairs are?

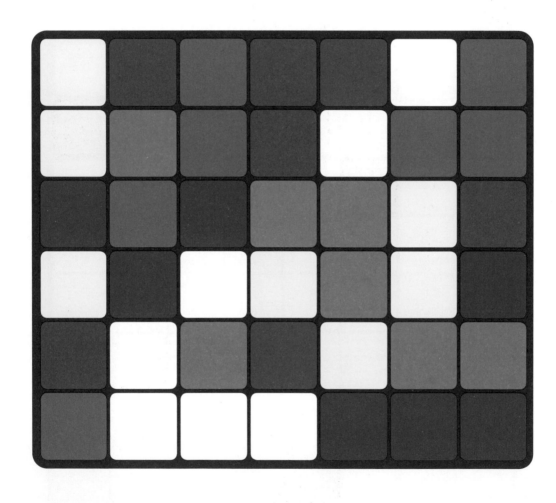

ANSWER SEE PAGE 137

2 HEXAGONAL

Which of the tile patterns A–F cannot be found in the hexagonal grid?

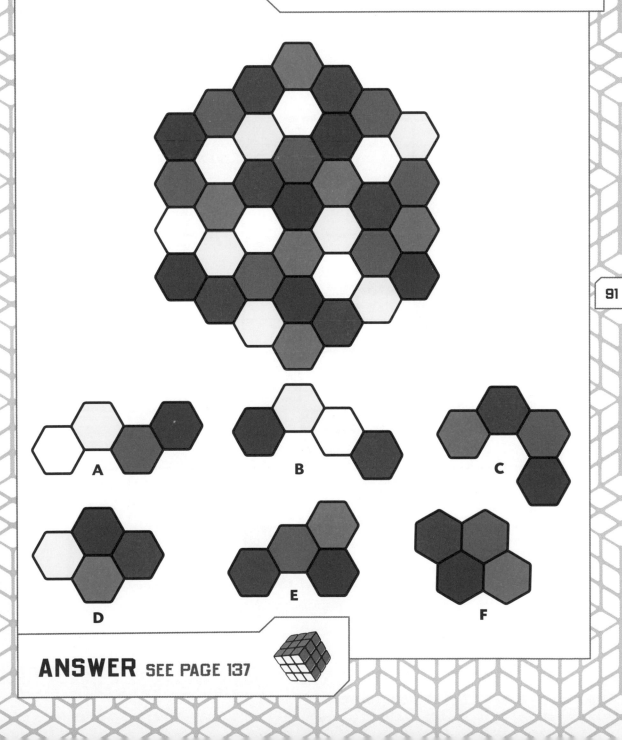

A

B

C

D

E

F

ANSWER SEE PAGE 137

TWO-TONE

In the grid below, each row and column contains exactly 4 squares of each of the two colors. No more than two squares of the same color can touch in a horizontal or vertical line. Can you complete the grid?

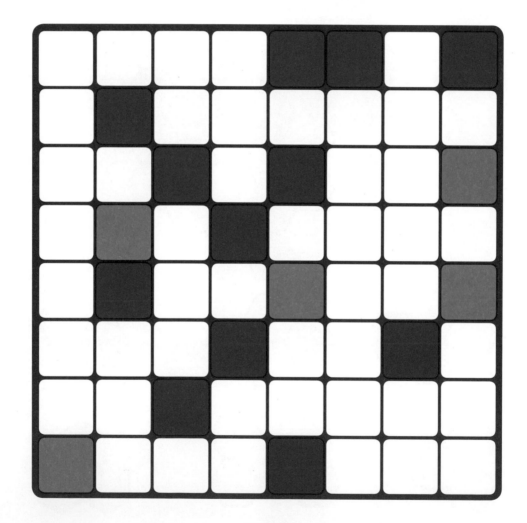

ANSWER SEE PAGE 137

EXPLODED

The pieces below have been exploded from a 5x5 square, where each row across is the same as its equivalent column down (1st column = 1st row, etc.). Can you reassemble it?

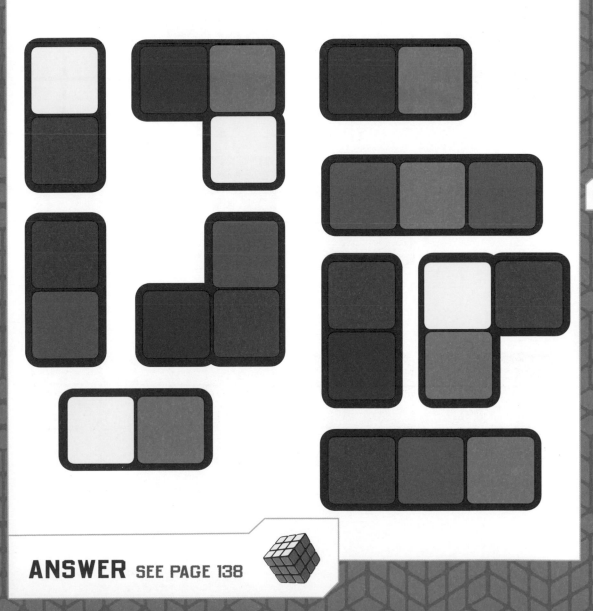

ANSWER SEE PAGE 138

NEXT UP

Which square A–D continues the sequence?

1　　　2　　　3　　　4

5　　　6

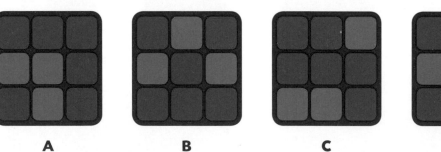

A　　　B　　　C　　　D

ANSWER SEE PAGE 138

ODD ONE OUT
Which of the squares below is the odd one out?

A

B

C

D

E

F

G

H

I

ANSWER SEE PAGE 138

88

7 TOTALS
What is the value of a red square?

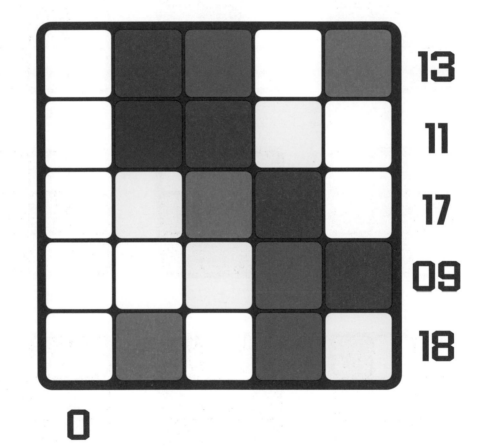

13

11

17

09

18

0

ANSWER SEE PAGE 139

89

PAIRS

The shape below is composed of 21 paired-square tiles, all pressed together. Each color is paired with every color exactly once, so one pair is white and white, the next is white and yellow, and so on, like dominoes. Can you figure out where the pairs are?

ANSWER SEE PAGE 139

CASCADE

In the triangle, each cell is the total of the two cells immediately below it. Can you place the numbers from the list below to correctly complete the triangle?

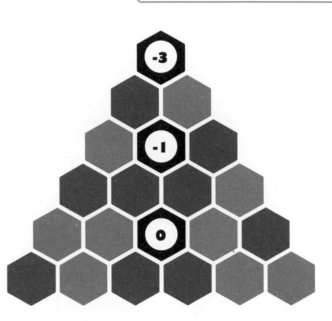

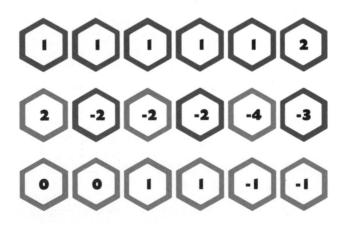

1   1   1   1   1   2

2   -2   -2   -2   -4   -3

0   0   1   1   -1   -1

ANSWER SEE PAGE 139

91

 6

TWO-TONE

In the grid below, each row and column contains exactly 4 squares of each of the two colors. No more than two squares of the same color can touch in a horizontal or vertical line. Can you complete the grid?

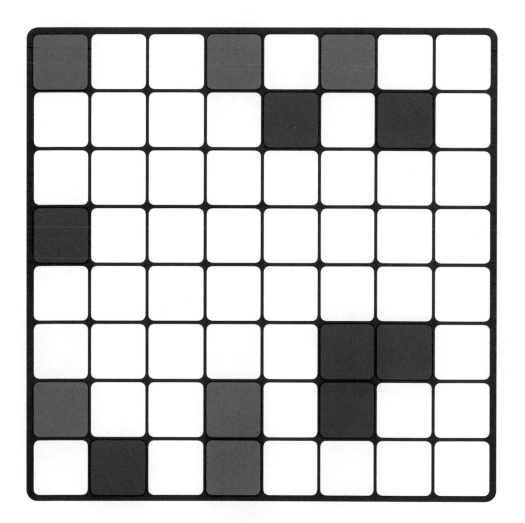

ANSWER SEE PAGE 140

EXPLODED

The pieces below have been exploded from a 5x5 square, where each row across is the same as its equivalent column down (1st column = 1st row, etc.). Can you reassemble it?

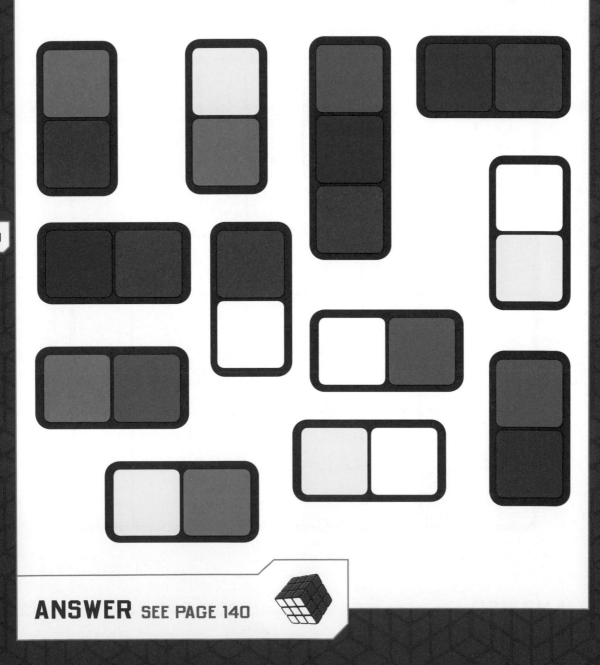

LINK

Join each same-colored pair of highlighted cells below with a path of the same color. Paths may not cross, nor may they double back to ever form a square of four cells of the same color. The correct solution uses every cell in the grid exactly once. Can you complete the grid?

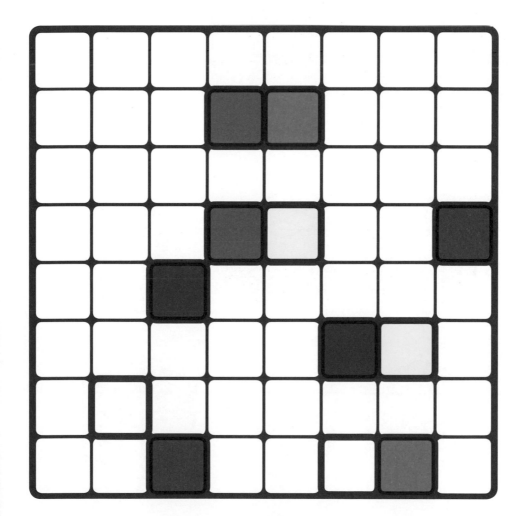

ANSWER SEE PAGE 140

94

5 CUBE MAP

Which of the Cubes 1-6 cannot be made from the Cube template above?

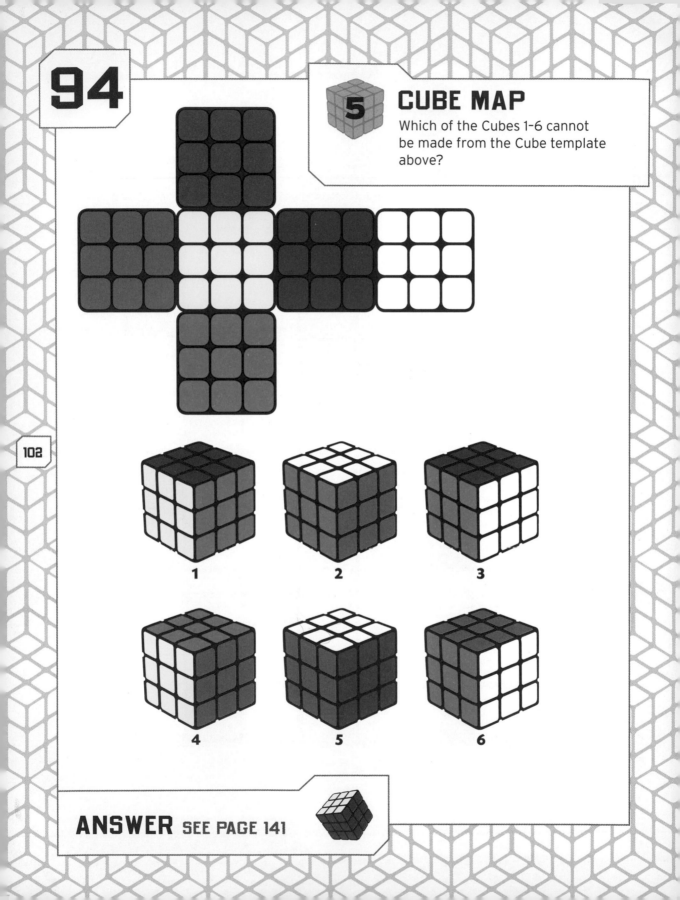

1

2

3

4

5

6

ANSWER SEE PAGE 141

4 BLACK OUT

Black out certain squares in the grid so that no color occurs more than once in each row and column. All remaining colored squares must form a group of two or more, with each square touching another colored square either horizontally or vertically. Black squares must not touch other black squares horizontally or vertically. Can you complete the grid?

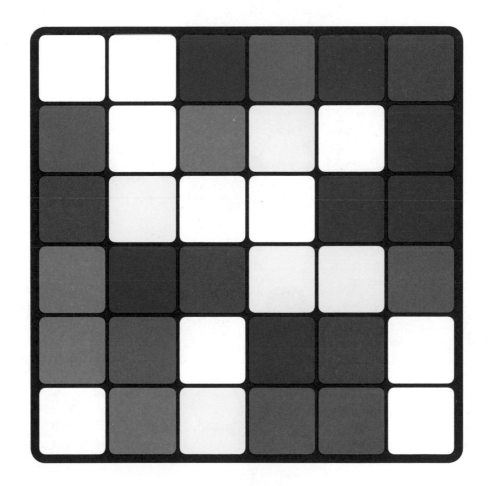

ANSWER SEE PAGE 141

2 HEXAGONAL

Which of the tile patterns A-F cannot be found in the hexagonal grid?

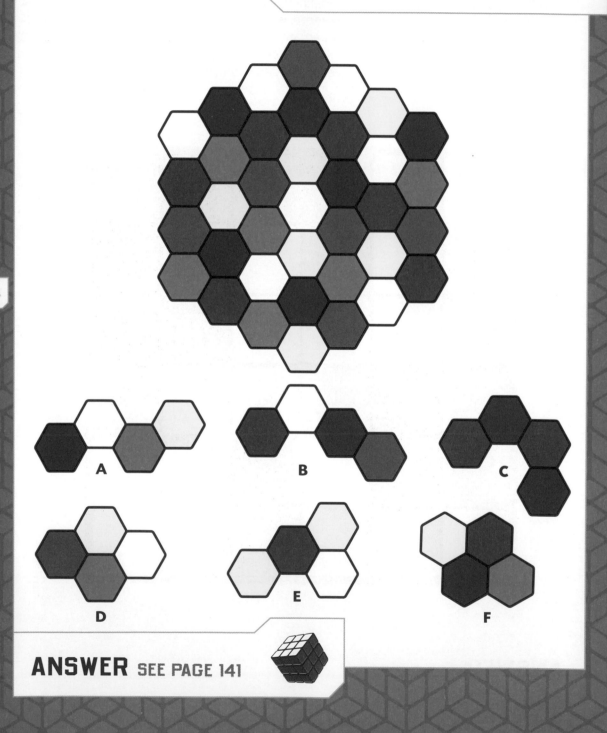

A

B

C

D

E

F

ANSWER SEE PAGE 141

MATHEMATICAL

The squares below follow a certain consistent logic. What value should replace the question mark?

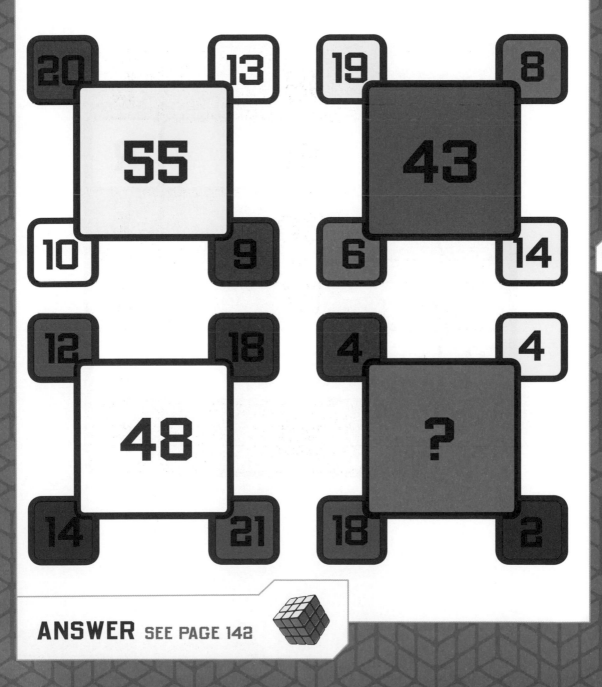

ANSWER SEE PAGE 142

ABSTRACTION
The diagram below follows a specific logic. What letter should replace the question mark?

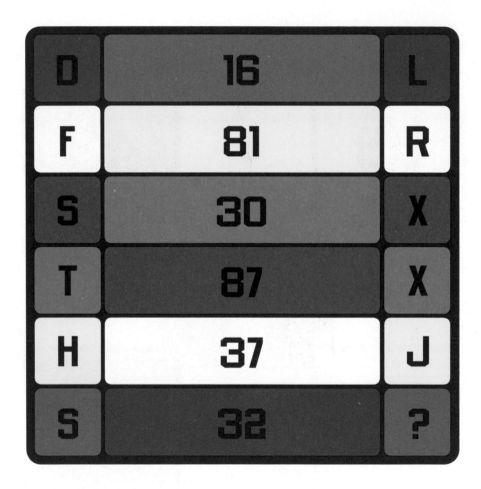

D	16	L
F	81	R
S	30	X
T	87	X
H	37	J
S	32	?

99

FACES

The patterns below follow a certain specific logic. How much is a red 3x3 square worth?

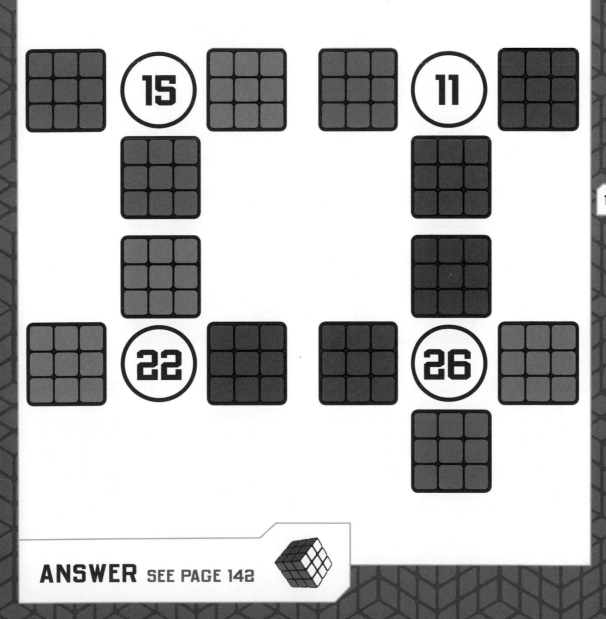

ANSWER SEE PAGE 142

100

FACE SEQUENCE
Which of the four squares below completes the pattern?

1 **2** **3** **4**

ANSWER SEE PAGE 143

101

9 ISLANDS

The grid below is divided into a number of groups composed of vertically and/or horizontally connected tiles. The numbers and colors on certain tiles below indicate the size of the group that tile is part of. No two groups of the same size touch each other. The whole grid is used, but not all groups are indicated below. Can you complete the grid?

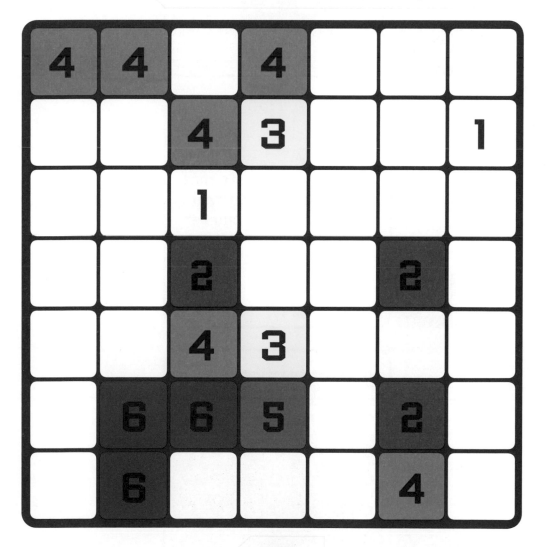

ANSWER SEE PAGE 143

1

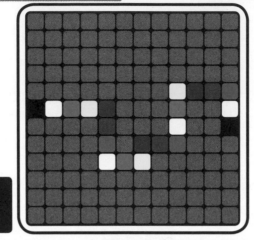

2

H is the only square that does not have a partner, having the same number of cells of each color (A&D, B&E, C&G, F&I).

3

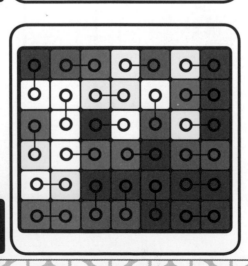

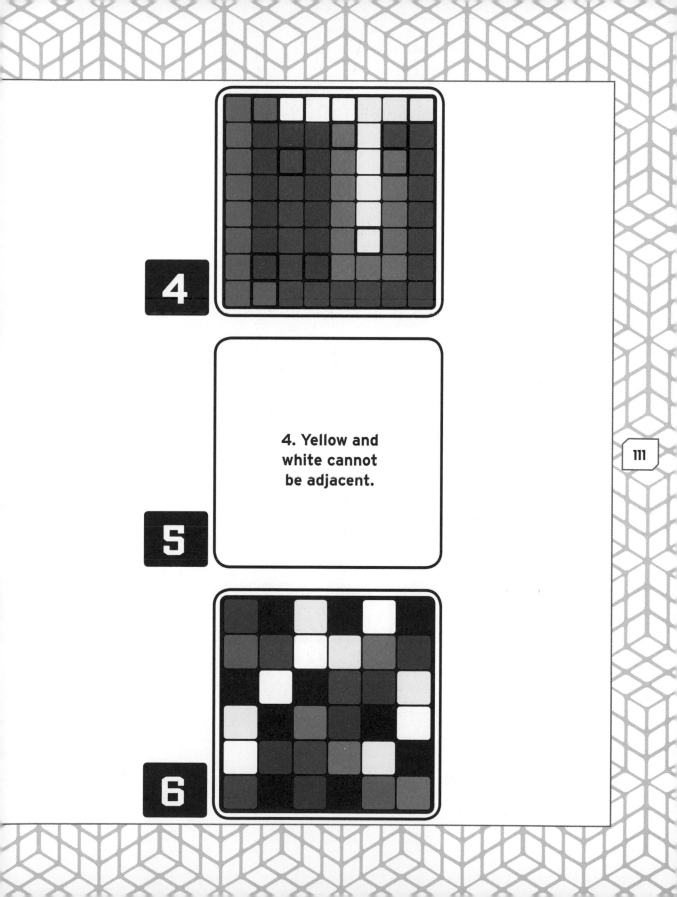

4

5

4. Yellow and
white cannot
be adjacent.

6

7

The 18th letter in the
alphabet is R.

8

9

10

A. The pair of complementary tiles is rotating counterclockwise.

11

Red = 1, Green = 2, Blue = 3, Orange = 4.

12

1. (Yellow starting top left moves 1 clockwise. Yellow starting bottom center shifts back and forth from right to left. Center alternates orange and green. Blue moves 2 counterclockwise. Overlap produces red.)

13

14

Center = (top left, top right, and bottom left numbers added) − bottom right number. 8 + 13 + 5 − 7 = 19.

15

E (the yellow should be red).

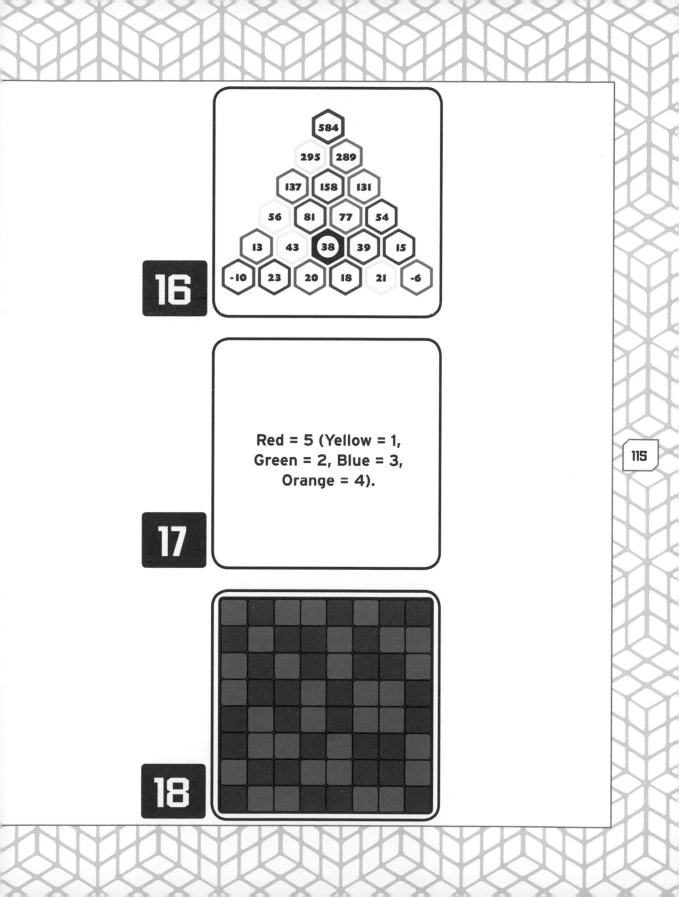

16

584

295 289

137 158 131

56 81 77 54

13 43 38 39 15

-10 23 20 18 21 -6

17

Red = 5 (Yellow = 1,
Green = 2, Blue = 3,
Orange = 4).

18

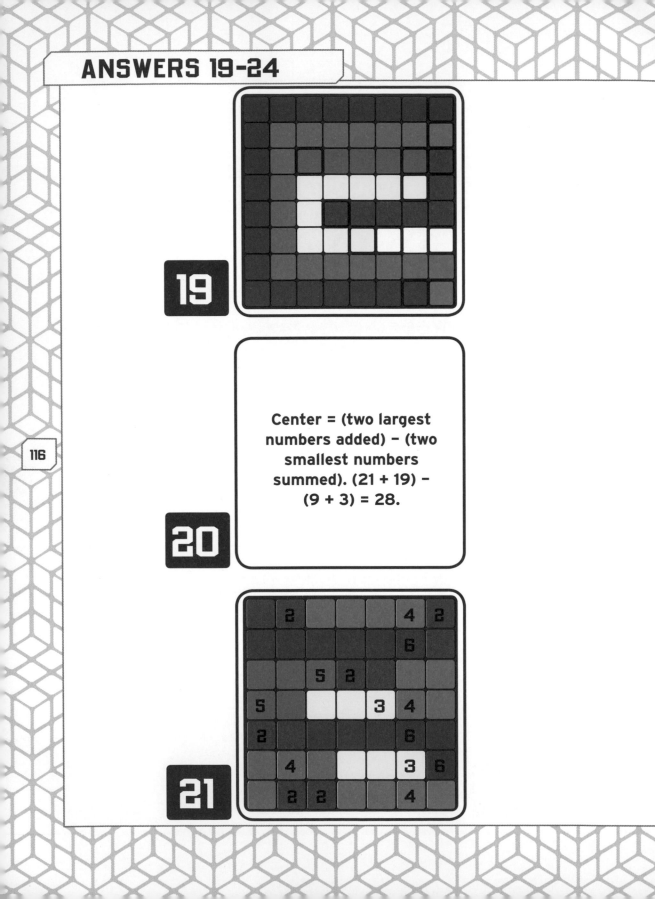

19

20

Center = (two largest numbers added) − (two smallest numbers summed). (21 + 19) − (9 + 3) = 28.

21

116

22

K is the 11th letter
in the alphabet.
28 − 11 = 17th letter, Q.

23

E is the only square that
does not contain at least
one tile of each color.

24

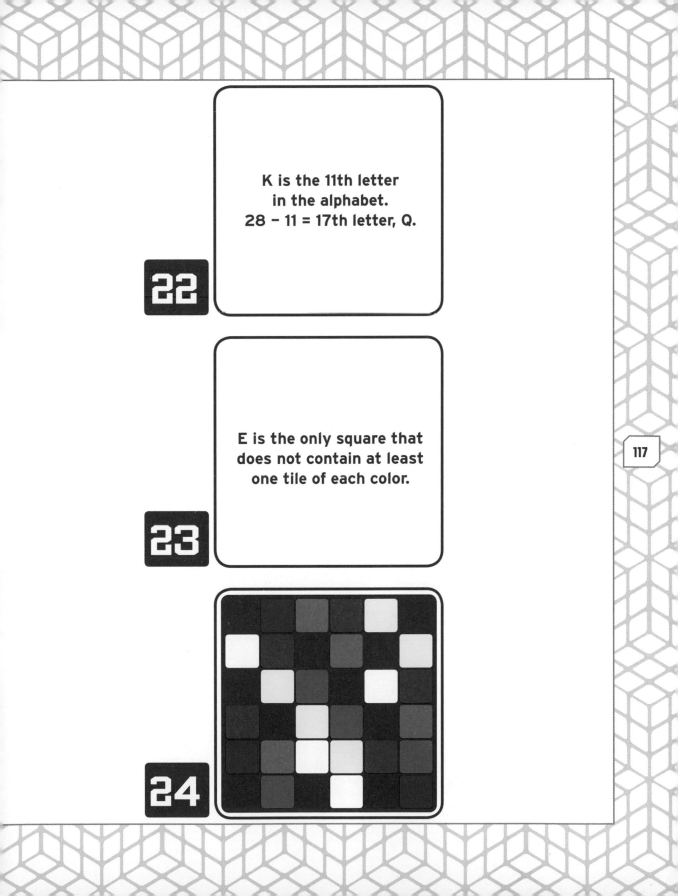

25

C. The complementary tile runs along the 3x3 grid from top left to bottom right, skipping 0, 1, 2, etc. spaces.

26

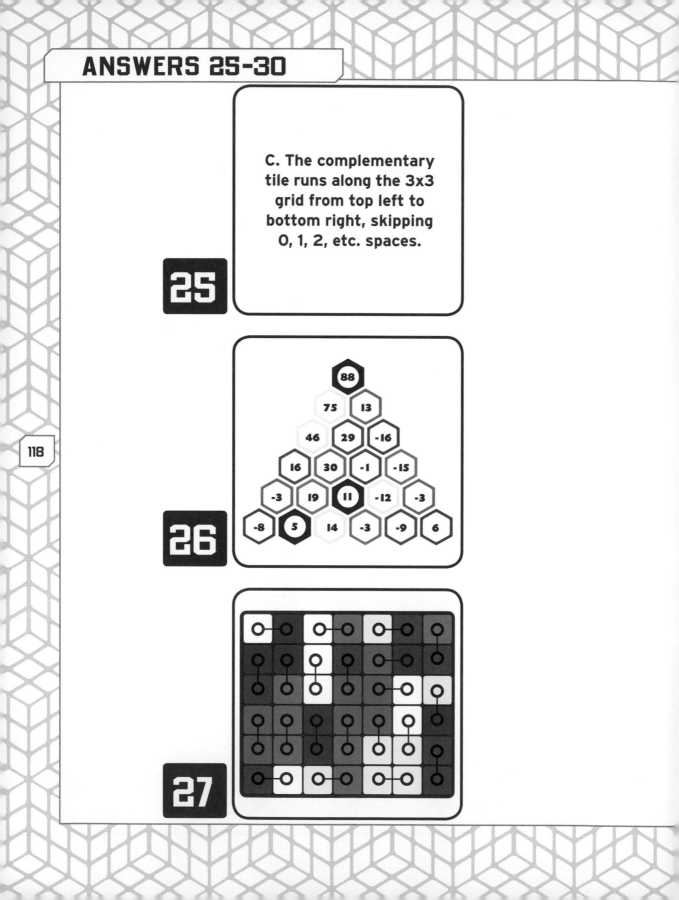

27

28

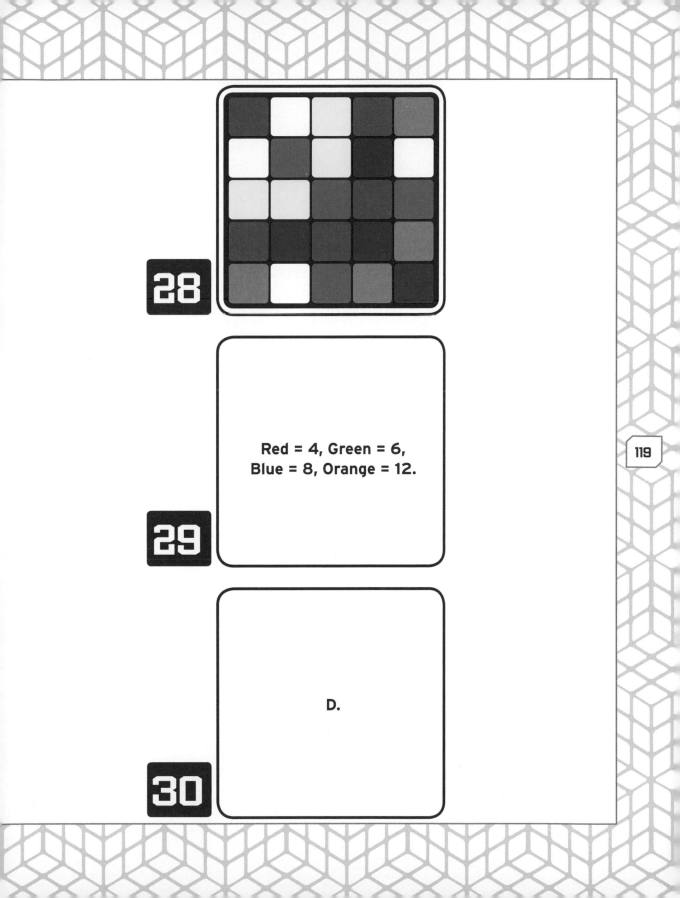

29

Red = 4, Green = 6,
Blue = 8, Orange = 12.

30

D.

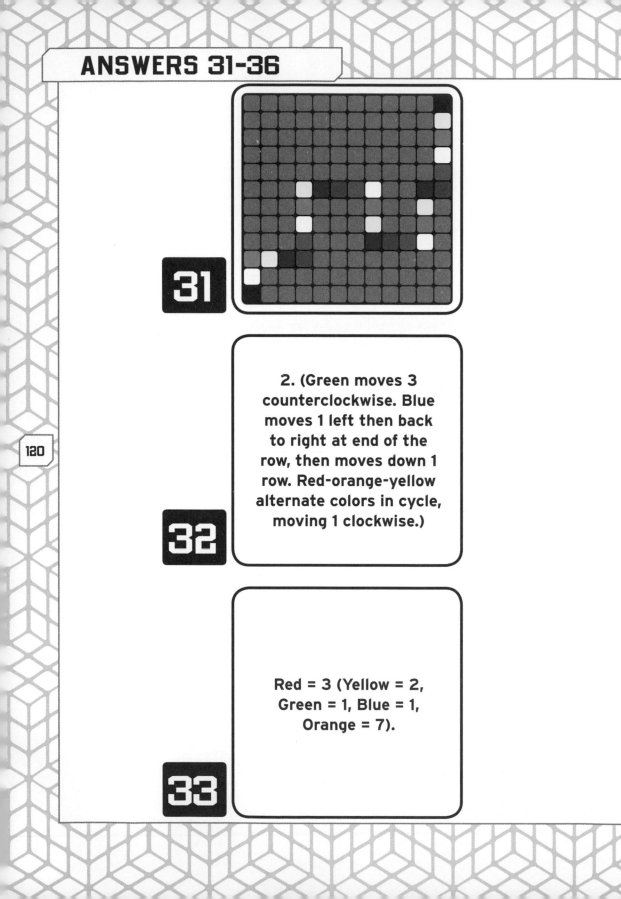

31

32

2. (Green moves 3 counterclockwise. Blue moves 1 left then back to right at end of the row, then moves down 1 row. Red-orange-yellow alternate colors in cycle, moving 1 clockwise.)

33

Red = 3 (Yellow = 2, Green = 1, Blue = 1, Orange = 7).

34

2. Yellow and green cannot be adjacent.

35

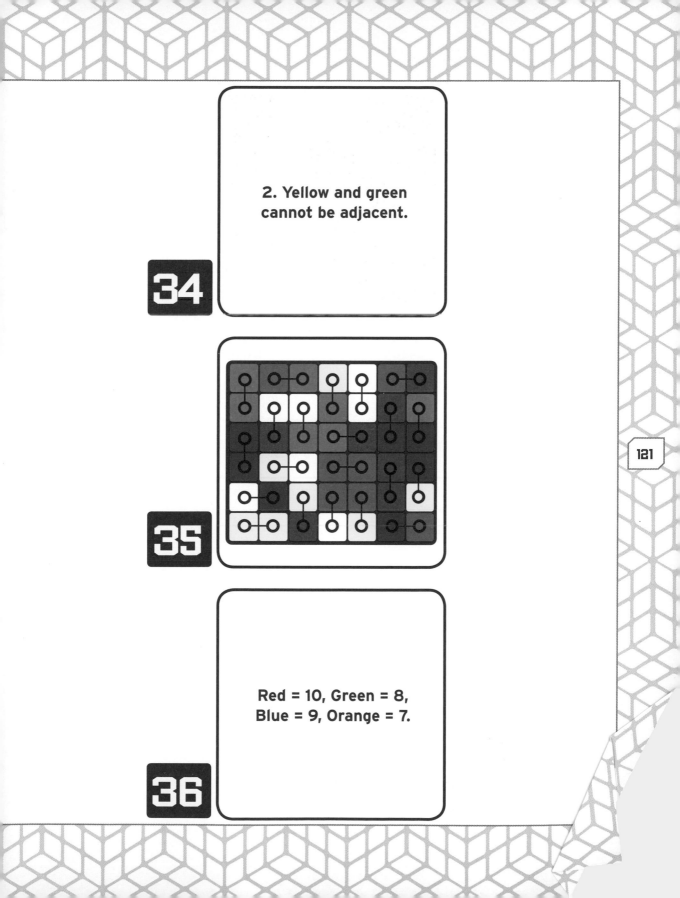

36

Red = 10, Green = 8,
Blue = 9, Orange = 7.

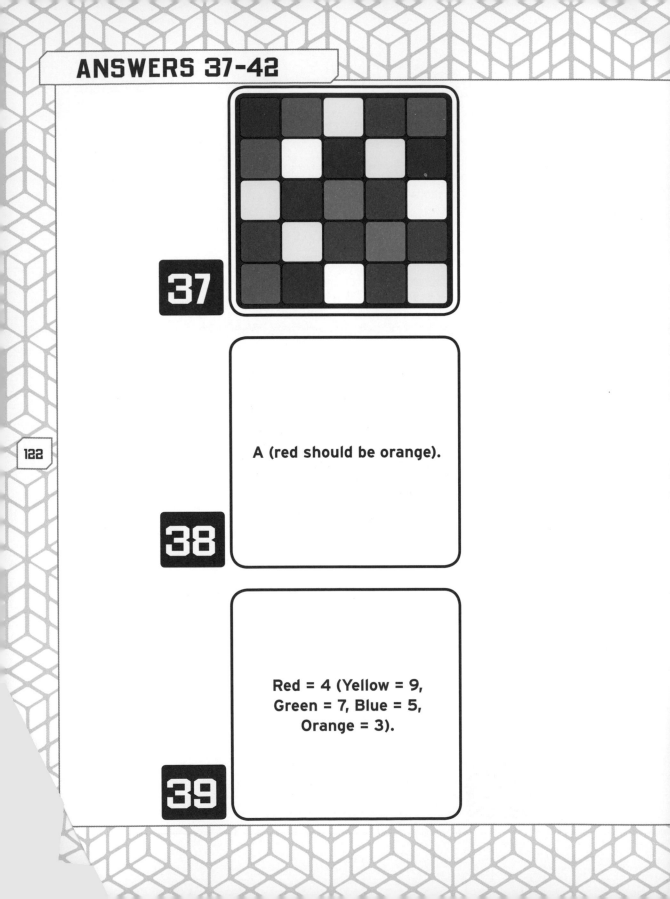

37

38

A (red should be orange).

39

Red = 4 (Yellow = 9,
Green = 7, Blue = 5,
Orange = 3).

4. (Blue moves 1, 1, 1, 0 clockwise repeating. Red moves top, bottom, right, left, center, repeating. Green occupies each space on 3x3 grid once. Yellow pair are always adjacent. Orange is as close to center-right as possible.)

C. One complementary tile starts at top center and moves counterclockwise one position. The other starts at bottom right and moves clockwise three positions.

41

42

43

Number = both letters' alphabetic position value multiplied. 120/6 = the 20th letter, T.

44

G. Taking the nine squares as a single grid, G breaks the pattern of the white-yellow-orange outer edge.

45

5. Red and green cannot be adjacent.

46

47

This is one possible answer.

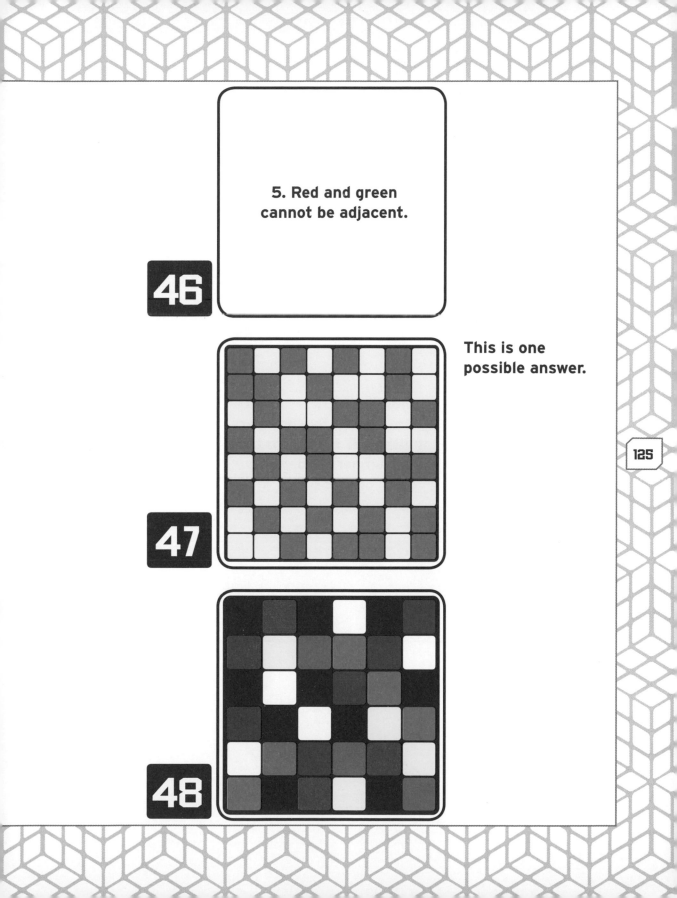

48

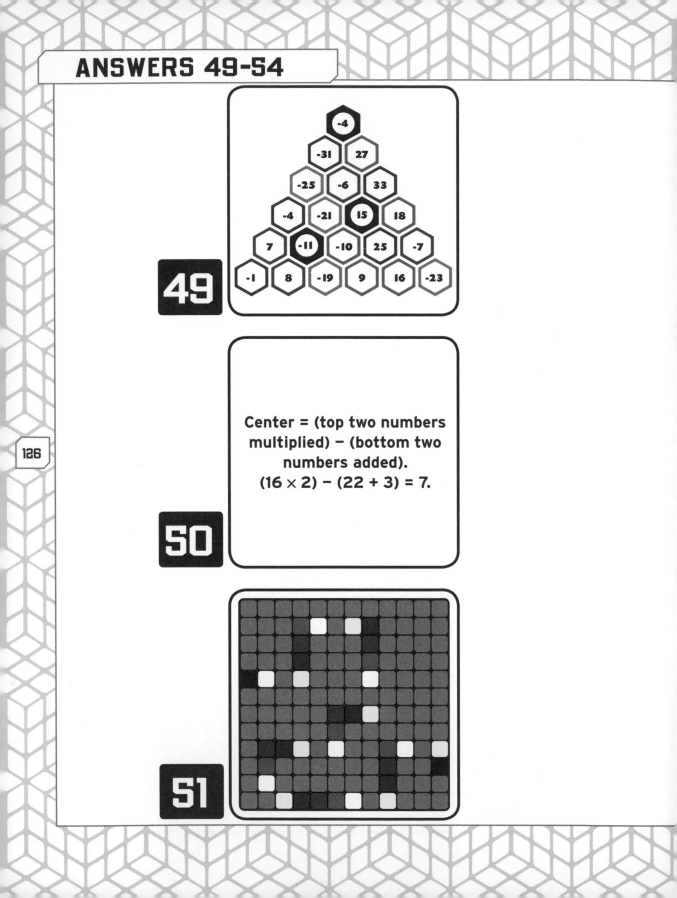

49

50

Center = (top two numbers multiplied) − (bottom two numbers added).
(16 × 2) − (22 + 3) = 7.

51

52

B (red would need to be yellow or orange, and move a sixth-turn inward).

53

1. (Both sequences alternate blue-orange-red-white in alphabetical order. Initial blue moves 3 spaces clockwise. Initial orange moves 2 spaces clockwise. Both sequences on same square cancel out. Center square is opposed base color if the two sequences are not adjacent.)

54

55

Red = 6 (Yellow = 3, Green = 2, Blue = 9, Orange = 5).

56

I. Each other square contains a number of yellow boxes equal to the number of strokes required to write its identifying capital letter.

57

Red = 7, Green = 5, Blue = 8, Orange = 9.

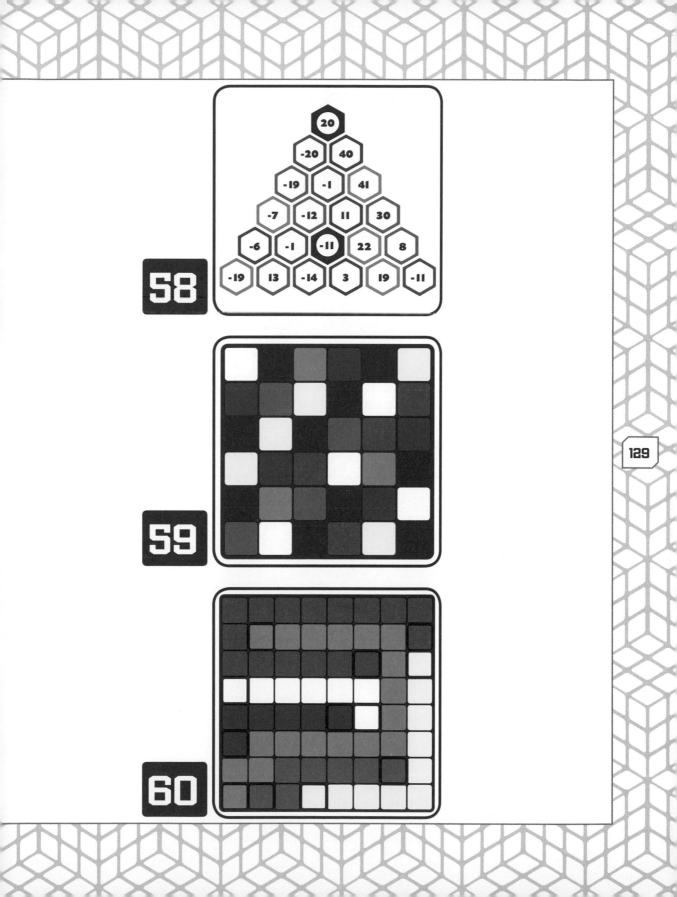

58

20
-20 40
-19 -1 41
-7 -12 11 30
-6 -1 -11 22 8
-19 13 -14 3 19 -11

59

60

129

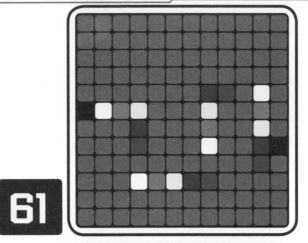

61

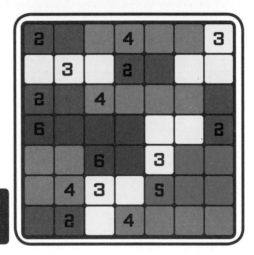

62

63

B. One complementary tile moves one position clockwise every other square. The second complementary tile moves two positions clockwise each square. The third complementary tile moves one position counterclockwise each square. Overlapping tiles retain complementary color.

64

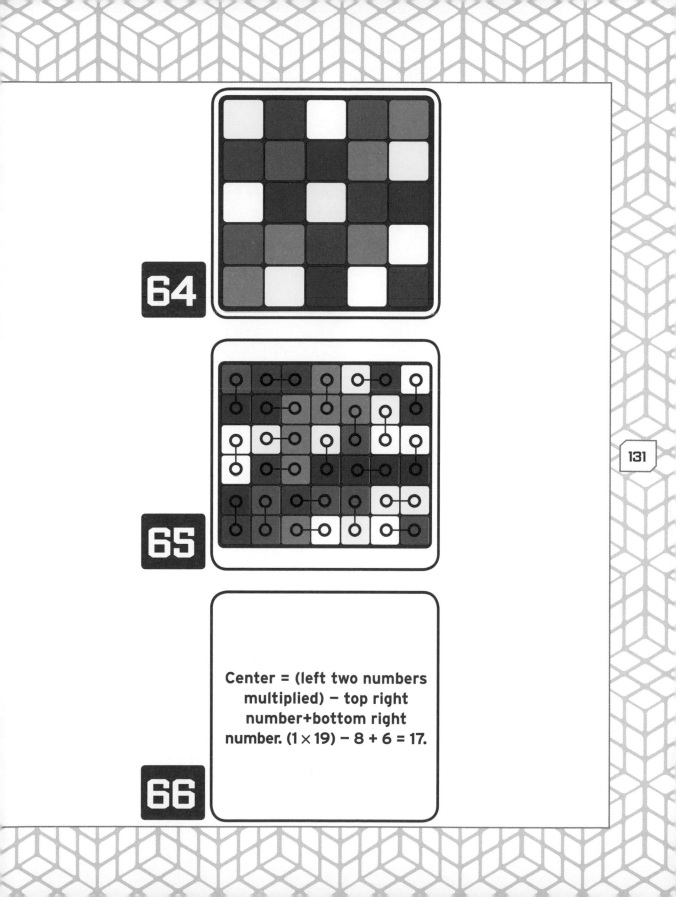

65

66

Center = (left two numbers multiplied) − top right number+bottom right number. (1 × 19) − 8 + 6 = 17.

67

3. With yellow left of red, blue must be on top.

68

The letters from top left form a sequence: jump 1, jump 2, jump 3, etc. Next term is Z. Numbers are random.

69

4. (Red moves 1 clockwise along top strip, returning to top left after top right. White moves 1 counterclockwise. Yellow pair moves two counterclockwise. Center is red on alternate boards. Any overlap produces orange.)

70

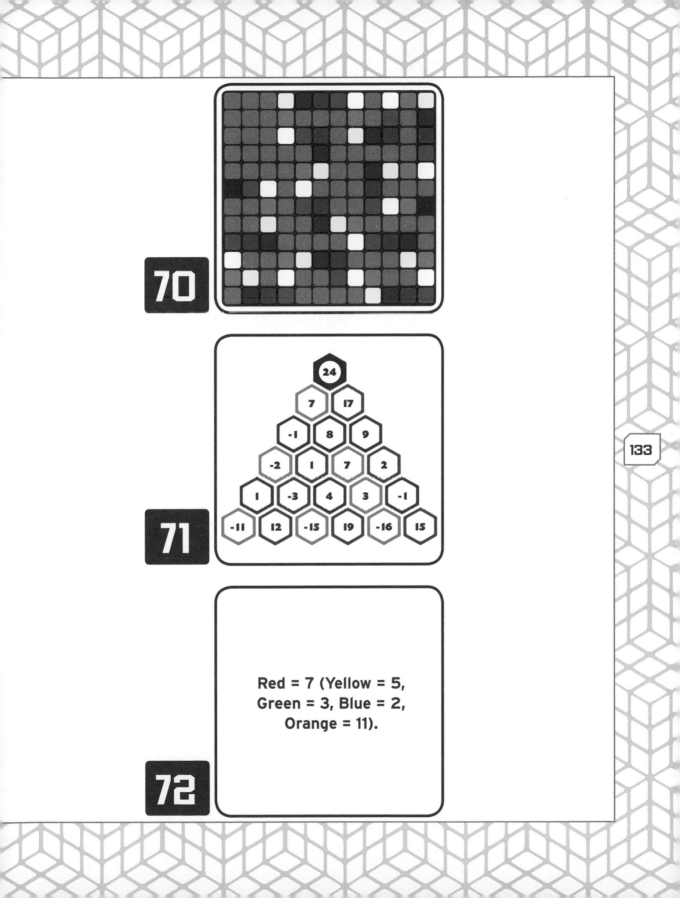

71

```
                    24
                 7     17
              -1    8    9
           -2    1    7    2
        1    -3    4    3    -1
    -11   12   -15   19   -16   15
```

72

Red = 7 (Yellow = 5,
Green = 3, Blue = 2,
Orange = 11).

73

Center = (top two numbers multiplied)/2 − bottom right number. Bottom left number is ignored.
$(14 \times 5)/2 - 7 = 28$.

74

Both letters' alphabetic position value added + number = square numbers in ascending order starting from 25.
$100 - (88 + 7) = $ 5th letter, E.

75

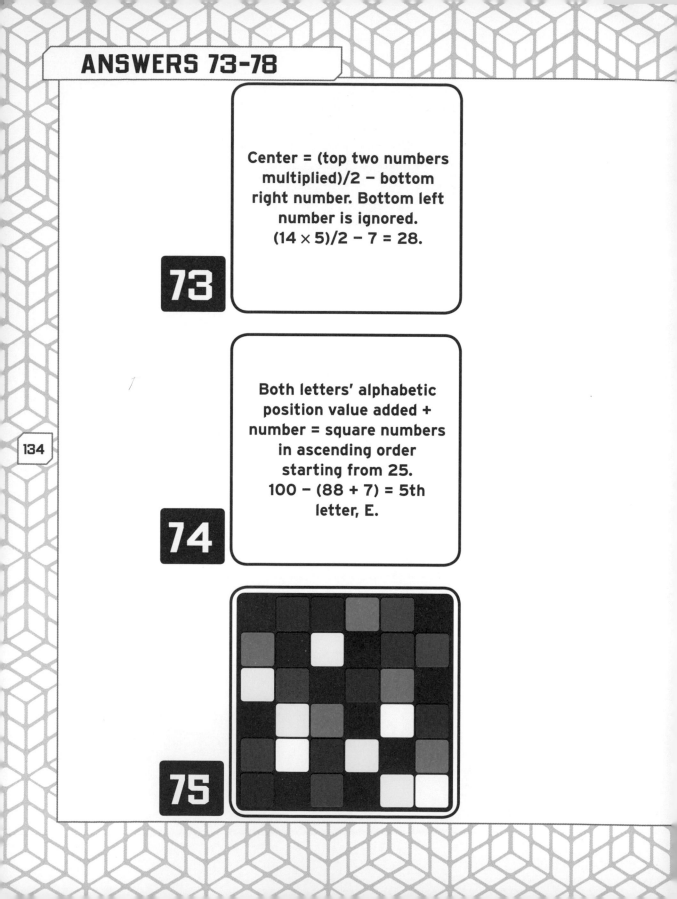

76

I is the only pattern not comprised of complementary (i.e., opposite) Rubik's Cube colors (green-yellow and blue-white were complementary on early production cubes).

77

4. With green on top, red must be left of white.

78

Red = 5, Green = 3, Blue = 6, Orange = 8.

79

A. If the tiles from top left to bottom right represent the digits 1-9, respectively, then the complementary tiles in each square in order form the sequence of square numbers, with A representing 36.

80

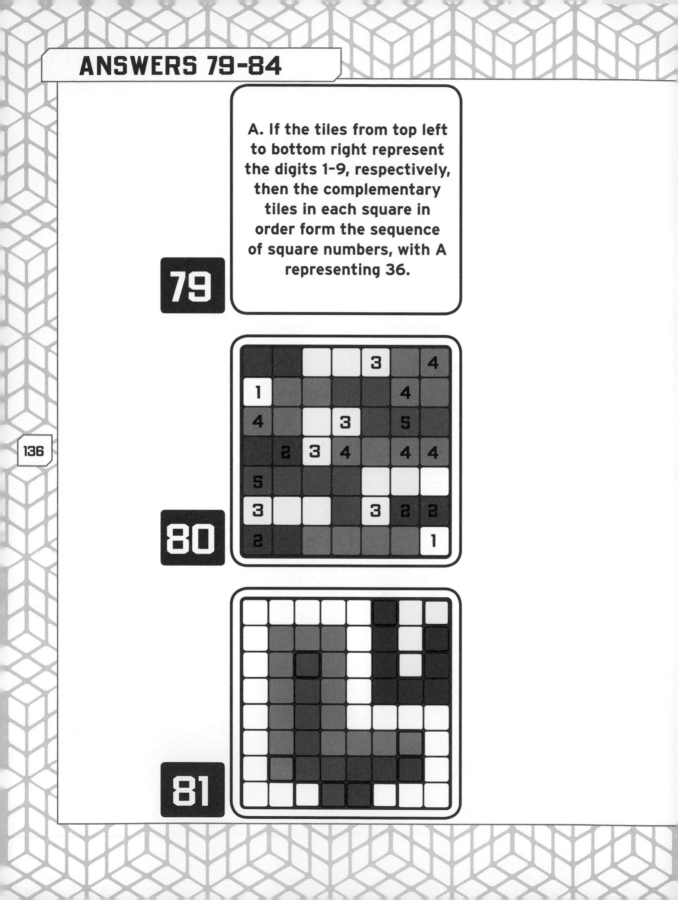

81

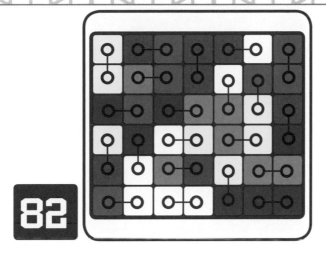

82

C (red should be white).

83

84

85

86

D. The complementary tile starting top left moves four tiles along the 3x3 grid from top left to bottom right. The complementary tile starting center left moves one tile clockwise. The complementary tile starting bottom left moves three tiles counterclockwIse.

C is the only square that does not have a partner showing the same number of cells of each color (A&E, B&D, F&I, G&H).

87

88

Red = 4 (Yellow = 6,
Green = 10, Blue = 1,
Orange = 2).

89

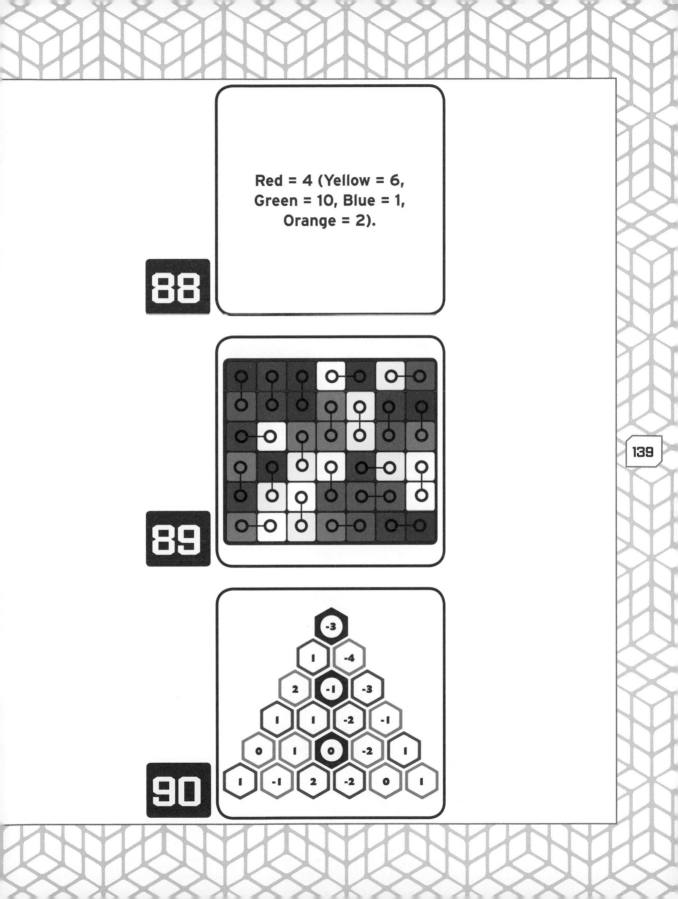

90

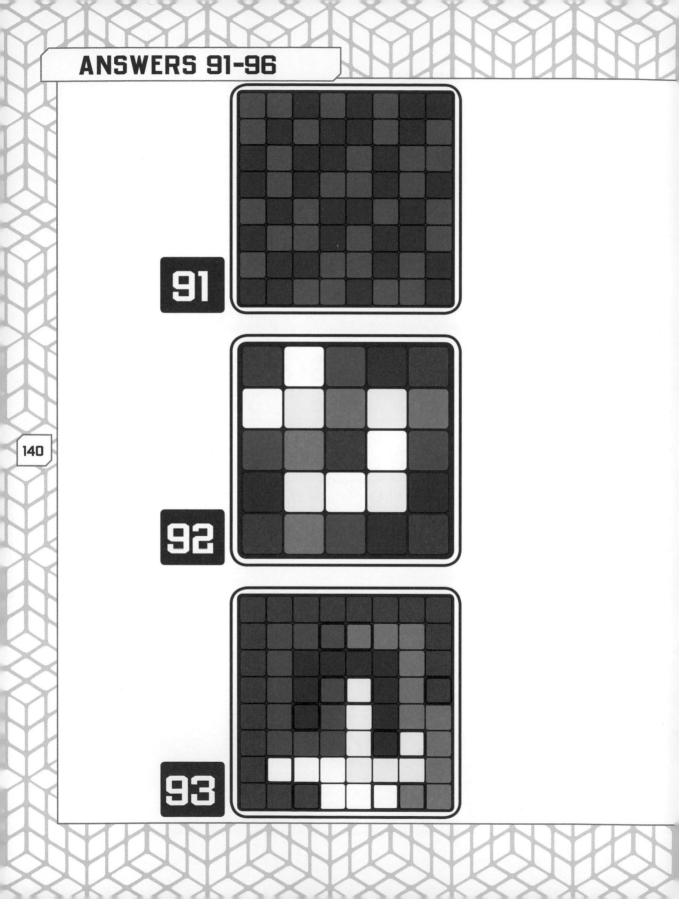

91

92

93

94

6. With white left of green, red must be on top.

95

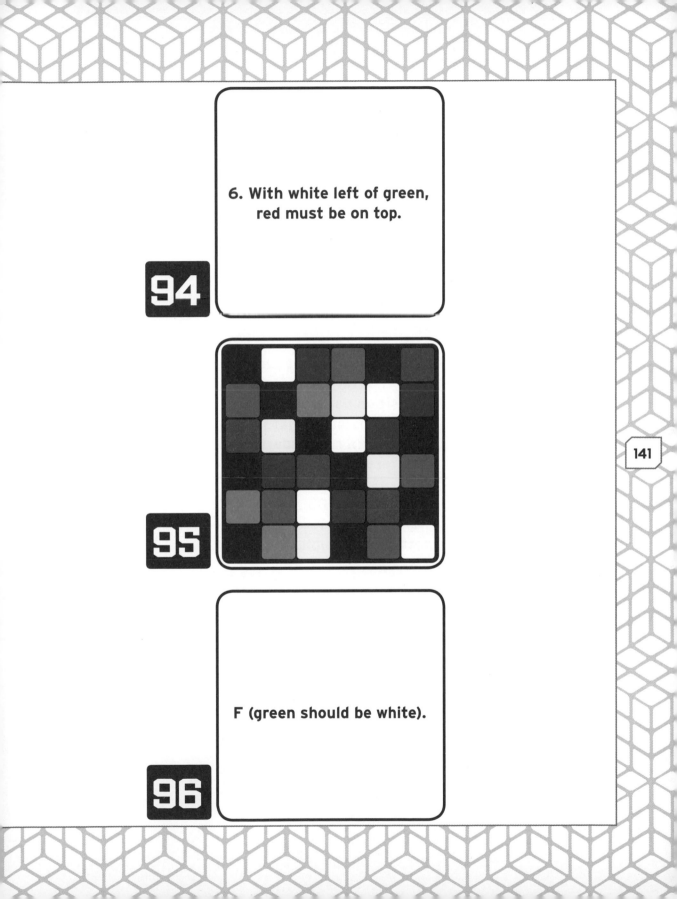

96

F (green should be white).

97

Center = the sum of the four numbers in the same position relative to their own center as that center is to the overall puzzle. 9 + 14 + 21 + 2 = 46.

98

Multiply number by left-hand letter's alphabetic position value. Perform long division (that is, divide with remainders) on the resulting value by 26. 19 × 32 = 608. 608/26 = 23, with a remainder of 10. The 10th letter in the alphabet is J.

99

Red = 10, Green = 9, Blue = 4, Orange = 3.

3. (Sequence uses all nine panels as a single grid, spiraling clockwise inward from top left, and runs alphabetically, blue-green-orange-red-white-yellow.)

4	4		4			
		4	3			1
		1				
		2			2	
		4	3			
	6	6	5		2	
	6				4	

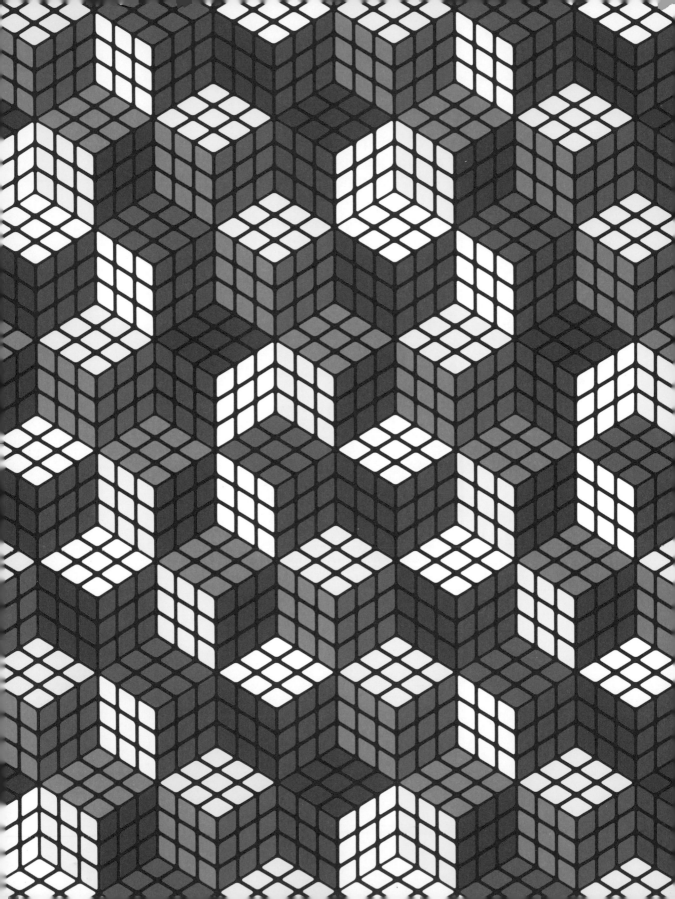